EDUCATION IN WORLD PERSPECTIVE

EDUCATION IN
WORLD PERSPECTIVE

THE INTERNATIONAL CONFERENCE

ON WORLD EDUCATIONAL PROBLEMS

CELEBRATING THE CENTENNIAL OF

VASSAR COLLEGE

EDITED BY

EMMET JOHN HUGHES

Essay Index Reprint Series

BOOKS FOR LIBRARIES PRESS
FREEPORT, NEW YORK

INTERNATIONAL STANDARD BOOK NUMBER:
0-8369-1962-9

LIBRARY OF CONGRESS CATALOG CARD NUMBER:
79-117814

PRINTED IN THE UNITED STATES OF AMERICA

Contents

Introductory Note

The International Conference at Vassar was a major event celebrating the centennial year of the college.

The idea of the Conference was conceived in 1954 by Mrs. Alvan L. Barach, then an alumna trustee and later chairman of the board. The idea was gradually developed by the Central Committee on the Centennial, composed of trustee, faculty, and alumna representatives. In 1957 an International Conference Committee was appointed, and in 1958 Mrs. George Washburne, an alumna, became its chairman. An Advisory Committee of twenty-six men and women, all experts in some phase of international relations, was appointed. Subcommittees of alumnae and faculty began work on planning for the conference, still four years in the future. As the time of the conference drew near, students and faculty were increasingly called upon to help.

The conference was planned and executed with the skill to make it an achievement in which Vassar can take pride— for it was done by dedicated, intelligent, and liberally educated amateurs. The experience of students, faculty, and alumnae working closely together on such a project was in itself enlightening and rewarding. An alumnae subcommittee successfully obtained grants to cover the entire cost of the conference. With gratitude, I wish to acknowledge the generous support of the conference by the following donors:

The Asia Foundation

Carnegie Corporation of
New York

Crown Zellerbach Foundation

The Danforth Foundation, Inc.

The Dearborn Foundation

Mrs. Bayard Dodge

Socony Mobil Oil Company,
Inc.

Esso Education Foundation

Great Western Champagne
Company

The Edward W. Hazen
Foundation

The Maguire Foundation, Inc.

Mrs. Eugene Meyer

Mrs. Jefferson Patterson

A few words cannot suffice to recognize the contributions of energy, imagination, intelligence, and plain drudgery by alumnae, members of the faculty, the student body, and the office and business staff. There were frantic moments, but the week-long conference went off graciously in an atmosphere of serious intent. It was a working conference, a week of formal and informal communication between individuals of diverse cultures, various interests, and opposing philosophies. The presence of some two hundred eager students who gave up a week of their spring vacation to be a part of the conference added special zest to the occasion. A sophomore commented to a member of the college administration who had worked for four years on the conference, "I don't see why Vassar doesn't have one of these every year. It's been the best thing we've had ever."

Some of the credit for the enthusiasm demonstrated by students and members of the faculty must go to the faculty committee that organized a series of preliminary seminars around each topic to be presented at the conference. During the conference these seminar participants were given opportunity to meet informally with our foreign guests for unhurried and animated discussion. At the close of the conference the seminar group met again to evaluate the conference from the point of view of the students. The faculty leaders reported that if nothing else the International Conference had been an educational experience never to be forgotten.

When the buses were loading in front of Alumnae House to transport Vassar's distinguished guests from all over the world back to New York, it was apparent that conference participants shared the enthusiasm that permeated the campus. Their week had been one of strenuous work, but the thoughtful and gracious hospitality of Alumnae House had engendered the friendly and warm climate for free interchange of ideas.

This book, *Education in World Perspective,* ably edited by Emmet John Hughes, will bring to its readers some idea of content of the conference. The meat is here. The flavor and spirit are in the hearts and memories of those of us who were privileged to work for the conference and to be present at its formal and informal sessions.

SARAH GIBSON BLANDING

Participants in the International Conference

ANWAR G. AHMED, political and welfare leader in Pakistan, was born and educated in India. She is vice president of the International Alliance of Women and the All Pakistan Women's Association; president of the Pakistan Conference of Social Work. Begum Ahmed is a former member for Pakistan of the United Nations Commission on the Status of Women.

HANNAH ARENDT, political philosopher and author, was born and educated in Germany, receiving her doctorate from Heidelberg. She came to the United States in 1940. She has been visiting professor in political science at Columbia, Princeton, and Northwestern universities. Dr. Arendt's books include *The Origins of Totalitarianism* and *The Human Condition.*

JOYCE PHILLIPS AUSTIN, state offical and lawyer, was admitted to the New York State Bar in 1946. She served as advisor to Office of Price Stabilization from 1951 to 1953 and as executive secretary of the New York Woman's Council, New York State Department of Commerce from 1956 to 1957, and is now assistant to the Mayor of New York City.

ANN ECKELS BAILIE, physicist, was born in New Hampshire and received her B.A. from Middlebury College. Mrs. Bailie is at present working with the National Aeronautics and Space Administration Board. Her specialty is celestial mechanics, and her calculations in the International Geophysical Year led to the discovery of the earth's pear shape.

MARGARET BALLINGER, member of Parliament, was born in Scotland and was founder and first leader of the Liberal Party in the Union of South Africa. Mrs. Ballinger was educated at the Cape University and Somerville College, Oxford. From 1920 to 1935 she was senior lecturer in history at the University of Witwatersrand. She was appointed in 1961 for a year as an associate of Nuffield College, Oxford, to write a book on her political experiences.

FREDERICA PISEK BARACH, editor and educator, received her B.A. from Vassar. From 1925 to 1929 she was on the editorial staff of *Golden Book Magazine*. She later taught creative writing at Sarah Lawrence College and from 1948 to 1956 was associate professor of English at Barnard. Currently Mrs. Barach was chairman of Vassar's Board of Trustees from 1951 to 1961.

LEONA BAUMGARTNER, public health authority, has been Commissioner of Health for New York City since 1954. Dr. Baumgartner received her M.D. and Ph.D. in public health from Yale. She has lectured at Columbia, Cornell, and Harvard and advised on public health to the ministries of France and India, to the World Health Organization, and to several government bureaus.

PARVIN BIRJANDI, psychologist, was one of the first women B.A.'s graduated in Tehran. She was a Fulbright scholar to the University of Denver and there earned her M.A. and Ph.D. in clinical psychology. She is the dean of women and professor of psychology and child guidance at the University of Tehran.

SARAH GIBSON BLANDING was born in Kentucky. She received degrees from Kentucky and Columbia universities and studied at the London School of Economics. Miss Blanding taught political science at Kentucky and was dean of women from 1926 to 1941. From 1941 to 1946 she was director and then dean of New York State College of Home Economics, Cornell University. Miss Blanding became the first woman president of Vassar College in 1946.

LAURA BORNHOLDT, historian and educator, graduated from Smith College with highest honors in history, then continued her graduate studies at Smith and Yale. Dr. Bornholdt was formerly a lecturer and dean of women at the University of Pennsylvania. Dr. Bornholdt became dean of Wellesley College in 1961.

GERMAINE BRÉE, teacher and critic, was born in France and educated at the University of Paris. Miss Brée was formerly head of the Romance Language and Russian departments at New York University and is now professor at the University of Wisconsin Institute for Research in the Humanities. Her books and critical studies of French writers include *Camus* (1959).

RALPH J. BUNCHE, government official, was born in Detroit. He was educated at California, Harvard, and Northwestern universities, the London School of Economics, and the University of Capetown, South Africa. His career with the United Nations started with the San Francisco meeting in 1945; before that he was the United States delegate to Dumbarton Oaks. He was a member of the first General Assembly in 1946 and United Nations mediator in Palestine in 1948. Mr. Bunche has been U.S. State Department specialist in Dependent Area Affairs and is now Under Secretary at the United Nations.

VERA MICHELES DEAN, lecturer and writer on international law and relations, was born in Russia and educated at Radcliffe and Yale. She has taught at Barnard, Mills, and Smith colleges, and the Institut d'Études Politiques in Paris, and the Indian School of International Studies in New Delhi. Mrs. Dean is director of the Non-Western Civilization Program at the University of Rochester and editorial consultant to the Foreign Policy Association. She is author of *Foreign Policy Without Fear* and *The Nature of the Non-Western World*.

HERAWATI DIAH is married to B. M. Diah, Indonesian ambassador to Czechoslovakia. She received her high-school education in Indonesia and was graduated from Barnard in 1941. Her main interest and profession is as editor and publisher of the English-language newspaper *Observer* and also the family magazine *Keluarga*, which is published monthly.

HELEN FOGG, teacher and welfare worker, a native of Massachusetts, received her B.A. from Smith. She taught for some years at the Shady Hill School, during which time she was a volunteer worker for the Red Cross. In 1946 she joined the Unitarian Service Committee, for which she now works as director of Overseas Social Work and Education.

HELEN FRANKENTHALER, painter, was born in New York and is a graduate of Bennington College. Her work is represented in permanent collections at the Museum of Modern Art, the Whitney Museum, and Carnegie Institute. She has exhibited in one-man and group shows in both the United States and Japan.

JEANTINE HEFTING, Master at Laws, was born in the Netherlands. She received her law degree at the University of Utrecht in

1945 and from 1953 to 1958 was a member of the Utrecht City Council. She has been alternate delegate to the United Nations Status of Women Commission and active in the International Alliance of Women and the Association for International Legal Order. Miss Hefting was first secretary for press and cultural affairs in the Netherlands embassy in Washington from 1958 to 1961.

RAJKUMARI AMRIT KAUR, world health authority and member of the Parliament of India, was born in Lucknow. She was educated in England and in 1930 joined Mahatma Gandhi's Ashram and served him as secretary for sixteen years. Rajkumari Kaur was appointed Minister of Health in the first Indian Cabinet in 1947, with Communications portfolio in 1952. She has been president of the World Health Assembly and twice deputy leader of the Indian Delegation to UNESCO.

HELEN KIM was born in Inchon, Korea, and educated at Ewha College. She studied also at Ohio Wesleyan, Boston University, and Teachers College at Columbia. She was president of Ewha Woman's University from 1945 to 1961 and is president also of the Korean Christian Teachers Association and a committee member of the National YWCA. On four occasions she was a member of the Korean mission to the United Nations.

ELBA GOMEZ del REY de KYBAL, economist, received her B.A. from the Universidad de Litoral in Argentina and her M.A. and Ph.D. from Radcliffe. She was for nine years economics and political affairs officer at the United Nations, during which time she was an expert in technical assistance missions to Venezuela and Haiti. Mrs. Kybal has been senior economist of the Pan American Union since 1956.

SUSANNE K. LANGER, philosopher, was born in the United States and educated at Radcliffe. She has taught at several American colleges and is now professor of philosophy at Connecticut College. Among her books are *Philosophy in a New Key* and *Feeling and Form*. Mrs. Langer's special field of interest is esthetics.

AMALIA GONZÁLEZ CABALLERO de CASTILLO LEDÓN, diplomat and playwright, was born in Mexico and has been minister to Finland and Sweden and ambassador to Switzerland. She founded the Mexican Comedy and the Popular Education and Recreation Office in Mexico City. Sra. Castillo Ledón was four times delegate to the United Nations General Assembly and chairman of the Inter-

American Commission of Women. She is under secretary of cultural affairs in the Mexican Secretariat of Public Education.

HELEN DRUSILLA LOCKWOOD, educator, was born in New York. Following a B.A. from Vassar, Miss Lockwood took her M.A. and Ph.D. from Columbia University. She is professor emeritus of Vassar, where she was a member of the English Department and its chairman from 1950 to 1956. Miss Lockwood was associated with Bryn Mawr Summer School for Women in Industry and is a former board president of the Hudson River Labor School.

ARTHUR W. MacMAHON was for over four decades a faculty member of Columbia University, retiring in 1958 as Eaton Professor of Public Service. He has an A.B. and a Ph.D. from Columbia and has served as visiting professor at many institutions, most recently in Turkey and India. His publications include *Administration in Foreign Affairs* and *Delegation and Autonomy* (now being published in India).

MILLICENT CAREY McINTOSH received her B.A. from Bryn Mawr and her Ph.D. from Johns Hopkins University. Her academic career in New York City began in 1930 when she became headmistress of the Brearley School, where she remained until 1947 when she was named dean of Barnard College. She was president of Barnard from 1952 to 1962.

LAKSHMI N. MENON, government official and teacher, was born in Kerala State and educated in India and England. She was four times alternate delegate to the United Nations General Assembly and has been both a member and a chief of section of the United Nations Commission on the Status of Women. She was president of the All-India Women's Conference (1955–1959) and in 1956 a member of the Parliamentary Delegation to China. In 1962, Mrs. Menon became India's Minister of State of External Affairs.

ZAHIA AHMED METWALLY, MRS. MARZOUK, social and government welfare leader, was born in Cairo and educated there and in England. She has been active in recreation, rehabilitation, youth, and family welfare. Her publications include studies of social service organizations, women's status, and districts and services in Alexandria. She is now director general of the Social Affairs and Labor Department in Alexandria.

EUNICE MATTHEW, educator, was born in New York. She took her B.A. at Hunter College, her M.A. at Columbia, and her Ph.D. at Cornell. After establishing and supervising rural schools in Tennessee,

Dr. Matthew spent five years in Thailand, where she did similar work under United States government auspices. Following shorter terms in Laos, Cambodia, Vietnam, and the Philippines, she is now professor of education at Brooklyn College.

JAIYEOLA ADUKE MOORE, barrister-at-law, was born in Nigeria. She attended the London School of Economics and was admitted to the bar from the Inns of Court, Middle Temple. Mrs. Moore was Nigeria's first woman social welfare officer and is a former assessor and magistrate in the juvenile court at Lagos. She is now executive assistant to the general manager, Mobil Oil Nigeria Ltd., in charge of legal and public relations.

ALVA MYRDAL, sociologist and educator, was the Swedish ambassador to India from 1957 to 1961. She was born in Uppsala and educated there and in Stockholm. In 1934 she collaborated with her husband, Gunnar Myrdal, on *Crisis in the Population Problem* which is credited with directly influencing the social policies of Scandinavian countries toward family-centered welfare. Mrs. Myrdal is founder and director of the Pre-School Training College for Teachers, a former director of the United Nations' Department of Social Affairs and UNESCO's Department of Social Sciences.

SALWA C. NASSAR, physicist, was born at Dhour-es-Schweir and received her undergraduate degree at the University of Beirut. She has taught at Smith and at the University of California, Berkeley, while studying for her Ph.D. Dr. Nassar is professor of physics at the University of Beirut. Her specialty is cosmic rays.

MABEL NEWCOMER, economist and tax authority, was born in Illinois. She is professor emeritus of Vassar, where she joined the Department of Economics in 1917. Miss Newcomer was an official delegate to the United Nations Conference at Bretton Woods in 1944, tax consultant to the military government in Berlin in 1946, and in 1950 a member of the Economic Cooperation Administration Mission on German Refugees. In 1959 Miss Newcomer published *A Century of Higher Education for American Women*.

DAVID OWEN, government official, was born in Wales and educated at the University of Leeds. During World War II he was personal assistant to Sir Stafford Cripps and a member of the Cripps mission to India in 1942. Mr. Owen opened the first office of the United Nations in London. In 1946, he became assistant secretary general of economic affairs, and since 1952 has been executive chairman of the United Nations' Technical Assistance Board.

ROSEMARY PARK, educator, was born in Massachusetts, is a Radcliffe graduate, and took her Ph.D. at the University of Cologne. In 1947 Miss Park became president of Connecticut College, which she had joined as an instructor in German. She is member, director, or advisor to education and community organizations, both private and for local, state, and national governments. In 1962, she was appointed president of Barnard College.

HELGA PEDERSEN, judge, was born in Denmark and took her law degree at Copenhagen University. After ten years in the Department of Justice, Judge Pedersen received a royal appointment to the Court of Appeal and later to the City Court of Copenhagen. She was Minister of Justice and cabinet member from 1950 to 1953 and is now a member of Parliament for the Liberal Party.

MYRA ROPER, born in Yorkshire, received her Diploma of Education from the University of London. She taught English in Canada and England from 1934 to 1938. From 1939 to 1942 she was assistant education officer of the Wiltshire County Council. Dr. Roper was principal of Melbourne University Women's College from 1947 to 1961.

ELISABETH SCHWARZHAUPT, lawyer and political leader, was born in Frankfurt-am-Main and studied at Berlin University. She has served as judge, legal advisor of the Counseling Office for Women, and legal advisor to the Evangelical Church of Germany. She is a member of the German Federal Parliament and the first woman to be deputy floor leader for the Christian Democratic Party. In 1961, Dr. Schwarzhaupt became Minister of Public Health.

CAROLINE K. SIMON, lawyer, received her LL.B. from New York University Law School. Her special interest is crime prevention and problems of women's and children's courts. She is a former member of the Commission on Discrimination in Employment, the State War Council, a former commissioner of the New York State Workmen's Compensation Board, and the National Probation and Parole Association. Mrs. Simon is now Secretary of State of New York.

LALA SPAJIC was born in Belgrade. She studied at the Belgrade Academy of Music and in Paris. Her songs and musical compositions have been broadcast in Yugoslavia and abroad. Mrs. Spajic is now assistant musical director of the Foreign Relations Department of the Belgrade Radio-Television.

KETTY A. STASSINOPOULOU, author, painter, and educator, was born in Athens and studied at the Sorbonne. She has been chairman since 1956 of the YWCA School for Social Workers and chairman also of the Greek Branch of Social Service. Mrs. Stassinopoulou is a long-time member of the Permanent Committee, International Conference of Social Work.

ALINA SZUMLEWICZ, biochemist, was born in Poland. She received her doctorate from the University of Warsaw and has worked with the National Malaria Service and the National Department of Rural Endemic Disease in Brazil. Dr. Szumlewicz has published extensively in the fields of immunology and tropic diseases. She is now on a fellowship to Johns Hopkins University.

BARBARA WARD, LADY JACKSON, economist and political analyst, was born in York, England, and took a degree with first honors in philosophy, politics, and economics at Somerville College, Oxford. From 1940 to 1950 she was assistant editor of the *Economist.* Her first book, *The West at Bay,* was published in 1948; her latest, *The Rich Nations and the Poor Nations,* was published in 1962. Lady Jackson is now visiting lecturer at Harvard in the Department of Economics.

EUDORA WELTY, author, was born in Mississippi and received her B.A. from the University of Wisconsin. Among her books are *The Robber Bridegroom, Delta Wedding,* and *The Ponder Heart.* Miss Welty has contributed to numerous journals, including the *Saturday Review of Literature,* the *Atlantic Monthly, Harper's Bazaar,* and the *New Yorker.*

Preface

The essential organizational facts of this International Conference are simple.

The conference, celebrating the one hundredth anniversary of the founding of Vassar College, was held March 19 to 24, 1961 on the campus in Poughkeepsie. It had been almost four years in preparation. Its participants numbered more than forty, from a score of nations and from all continents, and all but three were women. The far-from-confining title given to the discussions to which they were summoned was: *Emerging Values and New Directions, Their Implications for Education.* Specifically the participants were invited to range, in thought and word, across three great areas of discussion: economic and social developments, political relationships, and the relation of the individual to society. There were, in the course of the conference, eight sessions of general discussion—informal, casually presided over, free and fluent in range. And the substance for these sessions was essentially supplied from two sources. First, there was a major address on each of five evenings, before the assembled conferees as well as students and faculty of Vassar. Second, there were more than a score of relatively brief papers prepared by participants and read to the conferees before each session of general conversation and review.

The more subtle and important facts of the conference—its quality, its spirit, its scarcely articulated intent—are not so simple to state.

It was *not*, to begin with, a conference of educators. Its participants included lawyers and lecturers, members of parliaments and welfare workers, historians and health authorities—women whose fields of distinction ranged from physics and biochemistry to education and painting. They included: India's Deputy Minister of External Affairs, a senior economist of the Pan American Union, New York City's Commissioner of Health, the dean of women at the University of Pennsylvania, a former Minister of Justice of Denmark, the Swedish ambassador to India. Representing all parts of the globe, many religions, several races, and infinitely varied philosophic outlooks, they held one thing in common, the basic criterion for their selection: a proven distinction in their sphere of work—and a proven concern with the revolutionary world around them, its mortal challenges and historic opportunities.

The conference showed breadth in another way, too. It was not a closed conclave of selected experts, but a meeting enlivened by the participation or attendance of more than two hundred Vassar College students. This participation even preceded the formal conference—with nine seminar groups under faculty leadership discussing and debating the papers prepared by conference members. And the scores of students who gave up their spring vacations to share in the conference were rewarded with more than the simple chance to listen. They met—at mealtime, at teatime, on casual walks and in informal discussion groups of an evening—with the women leaders from all continents. These exchanges were free and far-ranging, and, as one appreciative student later wrote: "These were vital, interesting women, willing to exchange ideas with us. . . . This made the Conference a living, important thing to all of us, and the general impression left was one of thankfulness that at least the minds of the world can still act together."

As they "acted together"—as they met and talked and argued, frowned and applauded, listened and exclaimed—the members of the conference proved other things about themselves. They proved they could be crisp and incisive—and garrulous. They proved they could be freshly responsive to new concepts—and tenaciously bound to old ones. They could pursue lines of reasoning with great faithfulness to the original proposition—or with silent disregard of the last speaker. They proved themselves to be, in short, most remarkably similar to a conference of men.

They were notable also, as a group, for two things they did *not* do.

First: They did not set forth to develop and propose an elaborate pattern of conclusions, recommendations, or programs. They were there to exchange views—insights and perceptions, concerns and hopes, concepts tentatively held and attitudes reflectively entertained. Quite probably no one of them held hope of anything more from the conference than being a little wiser upon departure than upon arrival. Almost certainly no one left disappointed.

Second: This quite unusual assemblage of women, concerned with the role of education in the world, did not display the slightest self-conscious concern with education of women. The subject was alluded to only after several days of the conference had passed, and then most casually. Obviously, they thought of the matter (if they thought of it at all) as one so fully resolved, as a matter of sense and right so clearly established and accepted, that its mention could only waste words.

Matthew Vassar would have been most pleased.

E.J.H.

PART I

The Pattern of Discussion

The Pattern of Discussion

EMMET JOHN HUGHES

The words—and the women—bespoke a whole world: the divided but aspiring, confused but embattled world of 1961. Almost nothing fell beyond the range of their discourse with one another. How could it have been otherwise? They had come together with no intent more narrow than to think and to talk of the revolution in the universe around them—and of the tutoring of the young and the unborn to survive (and, hopefully, to create) in the decades darkly glimpsed ahead. And so, in terms ranging from the urgently pragmatic to the loftily philosophic, almost all things were spoken of: from international pacification to national pride, from crop control to birth control, from economic aid to mental health, from teaching of history to teaching of hygiene, from tribal taboos in Africa to juvenile delinquency in America, from training farmers to training astronauts.

Yet the most striking quality of the conference was something rarely made explicit, yet dramatically implicit. It was, quite simply, an atmosphere, an attitude beyond utterance: a sense of historic *concern*, a muted but manifest awareness that, in all the crises of man's story, the stakes had never been so high as in this living moment. The awareness was almost deliberately left implicit and unspoken. No one spe-

3

cifically talked of Hiroshima. There was scarcely direct mention of Soviet communism. There was almost a shying from allusion to the "Cold War." And yet, accenting or pervading the most casual or even banal phrase, there was the rather awesome knowledge, shared by all, that never before were men and nations compelled, by inescapable challenge, to *learn* so much, so fast, so well.

What was the sum—the serious nature—of all the speeches, the papers, the tens of thousands of words?

It was not a program of action. It was not a disciplined review of education the world over, in terms of institutions or methods or facilities or content. It was not even a logically planned exploration of the great problems confronting all nations in the sphere of education.

It was an exercise in intellectual *reconnaissance*, a patient probing at the frontiers of the known—and the edge of the unknown. It was a scanning (no more) of the terrain of tomorrow. It was a striving to see—and, a little, to measure—the summits to be scaled, the great chasms to be crossed.

The notes that follow suggest the glimpses gotten of this tough, troubling, but exciting topography ahead.

The Massiveness of the Challenge

The most peculiar perversity of the human intelligence is its suffering the greatest difficulty in discerning the thing most obvious. Obviously every participant, as she arrived to attend this conference, had long been aware of the obvious "importance" of education—and of the equally obvious complexity and subtlety of the modern world's demands upon education and educators. Yet it is almost certain that few, if any, departed from this conference without sensing that the "obvious" had become a little more clear—as well as a little more towering in size and in portent.

As the discussion of almost every hour made steadily more

evident, one could allude to no great fact or aspect of contemporary history that did not accent, deepen, and complicate the challenge to education. The political division of the world? Its serious healing is inconceivable except, ultimately, in terms of education. The intimate meeting of East and West for the first time in history? This can be a creative, mutually helpful and productive encounter—rather than a bitter clash—only as education makes this possible. The surge of the newborn nations upon the world scene? There is no way for them to take and to hold a position of true freedom and dignity in the world community—unless their leaders are trained and their people educated. The revolution in science and technology? This can mean nothing, and this can give nothing, to a people uninstructed in its use and its promise. The great gap between rich nations and poor nations, whose compassionate closing so urgently challenges the most advanced economies and societies of the West? Only as the rich are more profoundly educated in their responsibilities—and the poor instructed a little in patience as well as in the problems of others—will there be hope that time can be bought for the gradual closing of this fateful gap. The surging "revolution of rising expectations," as the least technically advanced peoples clamor for the rewards of industrialization? Uneducated, these peoples cannot conceivably have the skills and crafts to find jobs, much less achieve mass productivity. Uneducated, how can they even intelligently *define* their "expectations" beyond swift satisfaction of the day's material wants?

These explicit and concrete challenges would seem enough to establish as "obvious" the unique demand upon education. But—as the conference found itself discovering—there is more.

First: There is the fact that all the isolated and specific challenges to education are bound together as one by virtue of the interdependence of nations and cultures, suddenly sharing a common destiny as never before. As Barbara Ward sharply pointed out in her address to the conference, the revolution in technology—without parallel in all the millennia since the nomadic life yielded to the agricultural life—inexorably involves *all* human societies in the *same* profound transformation. ("All of us—whether we are of West or East, whether we are Communist or non-Communist, whatever our background, our culture, our history—are moving forward to the modern society based on science and technology.") Thus there is an unprecedented *universality* to the challenge. The issue is not merely the dependence of each part of the world upon education to achieve *its own* destiny. A common destiny makes the education of *each* area a critical concern of *all*.

Second: This universal and unprecedented challenge cannot be met by any static response, for the very revolutionary pace of our age makes today's answer obsolete by the morrow. Again, in Barbara Ward's words: "We are all experimenting with vast problems . . . Not an institution, not an idea escapes re-examination. All are being turned upside down, rethought, reapplied . . . There is not an area of life in which the forces of change are not fiercely, drivingly, unpredictably at work."

If all the great issues of the mid-twentieth century summon the resources of education for their solution, but if the very shape and form of these issues themselves keep pitilessly changing and redefining themselves—then are not all men and women, agencies and institutions involved in "education" required to undertake a self-examination as revolutionary in itself as the world they live in?

This, in fact, was the question gently but plainly posed at the first session of the conference by the session's chairman, Under Secretary of the United Nations Ralph J. Bunche. Urbane and reflective, yet probing to the most elusive question of all, Mr. Bunche observed:

Indeed, this is a revolutionary era. . . . I happen to think the end of colonialism may be, perhaps, the greatest revolution of our time—when one considers that, in less than a generation, more than 800 million people have made the transition to independence and self-government. We have seen revolt, too, and I think a real one, against racialism and racial stigmas of all kinds. And this, I suppose, has itself been part of the yet broader revolution in the aspirations and demands of all the underprivileged of the world, calling for a new and better life. But I wonder if it is not true to say there has been no comparable revolution—and perhaps no revolution at all—in the realm of education?

The question, of course, was—as the conferees quickly found, as they talked on—an envelope for countless hidden questions, including the meaning of education itself. And as the discussions progressed, these questions shaped themselves ever more clearly. What *is* education—as distinct from training? (Is instruction in the use of a tractor, the planting of wheat, or the irrigation of soil as truly a part of "education" as the learning of languages or the study of physics?) In utilitarian terms are there priorities in educational needs—mass literacy, general primary instruction, or a highly trained elite? But should education be discussed in such functional terms, as a tool for predetermined social purposes—or, rather, as the vital means for allowing the individual to attain his own full growth? (It was the intellectually lively and articulate Lakshmi N. Menon from India who reminded the conference of the crisp caution of Matthew Vassar: "I am not trying to reform the world, but to educate women.") And if education truly responds to the infinitely varied needs and traditions of each of the earth's regions and cultures, in what ways can the world community undertake its fostering or "internationalizing"?

Let it be noted immediately: None of these questions, semantic or substantive, was crisply answered, even by the end of the conference. Yet they were *asked*—with increasing concern, with frequent debate. And the asking quickened all participants' awareness of the massiveness of the matters they were weighing.

It was an American historian and educator, Laura Born-holdt, who, midway through the conference, most succinctly made the questions both personal and sharp. "Are we agreed," she asked, "on what educators are? Are they the agents of change, the innovators—or are they, rather, the conservators, the guardians of a culture? Are they the serv-ants of society—or its leaders? Are they *in* and *of* their society —or both *in* and *out* of it? Can and should they hold values that are not shared by their society? Can they be visionaries —reformers—even politicians—at the same time?"

Whatever else the conference may have failed to achieve in clarity or in conclusions, it could never be charged with failing to ask itself the most tough and elusive questions. So doing, it took some measure of the towering height of the challenge to educators the world over.

The Division of the World

The sense of the common destiny of all nations—and their common peril in the nuclear age—affected the temper and tone of the conference in a variety of subtle but palpable ways. Some of these ways seemed wise: a shunning of simplified slogans, an avoidance of prideful parochialism in ideas or words, a steadfast effort to appreciate new or alien attitudes or problems. Other effects of this general spirit may have been less constructive: an almost anxious muting of issues, with a logical loss of precision in their analysis, and an occasional readiness to close and seal a discussion with a tepid platitude.

The first, most explicit and most pessimistic, allusion to the state of world affairs came from Mr. Ralph Bunche. (It should be noted that at this time the United Nations was in the throes of the Congo crisis and its Secretariat had just been subjected to vehement Soviet attack.)

I am bound to say [Mr. Bunche lamented on the conference's first morning] that there has never been a time when the role of *truth* in the relations among peoples was so critical. I am not starry-eyed: I have never had great illusions on the place of morality in international affairs. But we seem close to reaching a state of anarchy in the world through a complete breakdown of international morality. There is an appalling loss and lack of integrity in position, in intellect, in utterance—in our international debates today. It threatens the existence of the United Nations—the use of the lie, the calculated lie, the reiterated lie. The Congo crisis has been a frightening demonstration of this. Optimist though I have been, my faith has been shaken these last months by all the stupidities and deceits and banalities we have witnessed through this crisis, compounded by outside interventions and tactical maneuvers of the Cold War. It has all been so intense and so incredible as to make one question, if only fleetingly, whether mankind can be saved—or really is even entitled to be saved.

The conference can hardly be criticized for refusing to get caught—and lost—in the familiar polemics of the Cold War. At its best it insisted that the great issues of modern history were deeper and broader than this conflict.

Yet—at less than its best—the conference seemed at times close to implying that the conflict of nations was not only secondary to grander matters but also was, conceivably, resolvable with a cliché or two. The vocabulary became on occasion slippery and superficial. The word "education" was sometimes invoked as a kind of miracle drug, with properties to cure the enmities and hostilities that (by inference) had no basis other than mere lack of knowledge or "tolerance." The word "rationality" was much favored by some, and—since it was largely undefined and therefore meant little more than an exhortation to be "reasonable"—the odd suggestion seemed to be that those who imagined great substantive

issues to be dividing the world were suffering mere superstitions.

As all this implies, the hope—the anxiety—for world pacification colored much that was said. There was quick and general
assent that "international-mindedness" was a crucial purpose
of education; and no word was used with more reverence—
or repetition—than "understanding." If different nations and
cultures would only *understand* one another—by learning of
their varying ways and traditions, perspectives and purposes
—there would be (it was implied most hopefully) a notable
decline in world tension and dissension. And this appeal to
understanding was perhaps stated most fully, on the final
day of the conference, by the American philosopher Susanne
Langer:

On the matter of acceptance of another's way of life, you cannot
accept what you do not understand. The problem of education,
in a world completely populated by people with different ideas,
is to make honest efforts to understand these ideas. The question
arises, for example, of the political intent, or the nefarious program, of the Soviet Union. But what is the *idealism* underlying
the Soviet ideology? As long as you will not admit that there is
any idealism there—that there may be something there not just
acceptable but even noble—then I do not think you can say you
understand it. And only if you really understand it can you judge
how far (like Plato's ideal State) it may fall from reality. . . .
You have to have a kind of international education free from the
fear of being accused of accepting an unpopular ideology because
it dares to look at that ideology from the viewpoint of its pro-
ponents. This freedom from fear must be instilled into international education.

In the spirit suggested by these words, it is not surprising
that there were some who used the word "coexistence" without much precision.

There were, however, sharp cautions also given by some
participants against the too simplified use of the words like

"understanding." Teacher and critic Germaine Brée, for example, punctuated one discussion particularly crowded with vague exhortations on "understanding" by observing simply: "It is fine to ask all of us to understand one another. Obviously, we have to understand a problem or a people or a culture *first*. But *after* we have understood, there can still remain crucial conflicts and decisions."

More extreme and explicit was the dissent of Elisabeth Schwarzhaupt of Germany—lawyer, judge, and Christian Democratic member of the West German Parliament. In her paper prepared for the conference, she took due note of the tendency of the Western intellectual to examine all social systems for relative good in them, but she sharply warned: "The more wholeheartedly we care about and 'accept' the individual who lives under a different regime from ours, the more decidedly must we condemn and 'reject' any state system that disregards that individual's freedom and privacy." Bluntly—and along with an assertion of "the Christian basis of our civilization"—she insisted there could be no trifling with the principle of "the rights of all peoples to live in liberty under the rule of absolute law."

It seemed hardly a matter of chance that the member of the conference most disdainful of any kind of philosophic neutralism—or a lofty detachment from the sharp issues of world politics—came from the nation in the center of Europe whose own division was part of the scar of a divided world.

One slightly intense ideological encounter marked the conference. It was interesting that this exchange was not provoked by any Western conferee's dialogue with a neutralist; it was, instead, a discussion entirely confined to a conversation among conferees from the Far East. The Indonesian conferee, Mrs. Herawati Diah, read to the conference a prepared paper on the "guided democracy" of Indonesia's Sukarno. Since, she explained, "there is no democracy that is not limited," it is both reasonable and "democratic" to insist that "a strong government" may better serve a people's needs and aspirations. In the general discussion that followed shortly, a written question from a student rather irreverently inquired: "How much do the people contribute to the 'guidance' in a 'guided democracy'?" A little haltingly Mrs. Diah replied: "I do not think I can comment on this. We have to, as a people, attain our objectives—goals we have not been able to reach in sixteen years of independence. This is why we are embarked on the new system. . . . I believe that the people contribute by not grumbling about what is taking place." The exchange that followed was gently forced by the two conferees from India —Lakshmi N. Menon and Rajkumari Amrit Kaur—and it went like this:

MRS. MENON: When we speak of a democracy, we expect certain things of it . . . How much of these things are available in a "guided democracy"?

MRS. DIAH: We have a parliament which has been—well, it was abolished and we instituted a new parliament. In the past, we were not able to work because of . . . the political parties, which meant we could not achieve anything. . . .

MRS. KAUR: Are these members of parliament elected directly or are they nominated?

MRS. DIAH: There are three groups that emerged from the election of 1955.

MRS. KAUR: Of those that had not been elected, where are they now?

MRS. DIAH: They are back in parliament—they joined other parties.

MRS. KAUR: Is there any opposition that may make its voice felt—either through the press or in public meetings?

MRS. DIAH: As long as there is a feeling for our revolution and our aims and our ideals, as long as we keep within those limits.

MRS. STASSINOPOULOU: May I ask if this party of the opposition is represented in the parliament?

MRS. DIAH: Not in the Western sense of the word.

The conference was undisturbed by any other such exchanges. Good sense and good grace dictated the restraint. At the same time an observer—perhaps a little troubled by too many imprecise appeals for understanding—might have been forgiven, once or twice, for frowning at the rather placid generalizations, as he recalled the wry speculation of historian Harold Nicolson: "It would be interesting to analyze how many false decisions, how many fatal misunderstandings, have arisen from such pleasant qualities as shyness, consideration, affability, or ordinary good manners."

This, however, was scarcely a peace conference. It was simply a conference of women, from all the world, whose every thought seemed a little haunted, a little darkened, by the world's want of peace.

The Role of Nationalism

If the conference occasionally found itself lauding international-mindedness and understanding and rationality as undiscriminatingly as if tribute were being paid to goodness and beauty and truth, it dealt more sharply and explicitly—and more abrasively—with the simple phenomenon of nationalism. What was meant by nationalism was not, of course, chauvinism, nor national insularity, but rather the sense and pride of national identity. And the discussion of—and dissents upon—the matter were made directly relevant to the purpose and the content of education.

Threaded through every day of the discussions, the issue was posed initially, and lucidly, on the first day of the conference, by the Iranian psychologist, Parvin Birjandi.

I would like to look a little longer [she remarked] at some of the questions raised by talking of internationalism. I wonder, for example, if a seriously international way of thinking is really possible without a people *first* having known an awakening of their own *nationalistic* spirit. My country—Iran—is going through the growing pains of sensing a new nationalism. Rather than being alien to the spirit of internationalism, may this stage of self-understanding not be a necessary step on the road to a larger awareness? It is so with an individual: A child has to grow thorugh certain stages of maturing. May this not be true of a nation?

And a little later in the conference Mrs. Birjandi restated her thesis:

We are talking about the cultivating of international attitudes, in our young particularly. Now it is a truth shown by all psychological studies that individuals who accept themselves become, thereby, capable of accepting others. Their own sense of identity enables them to see and to respect the identity of others. The same should be true of nations—with a national sense of self-respect being really essential to an international outlook embracing other nations.

By mid-conference this proposition was being subjected to debate. Both Germaine Brée and Salwa G. Nassar, physicist from Lebanon, tended similarly to stress that the learning of *one* national history or *one* language endowed the individual with the intellectual tools for more general learning —and the implication clearly was that knowledge-in-depth of one's own national traditions did, in fact, better equip one for citizenship in the world community. Editor and author Vera Micheles Dean took issue.

I must challenge that point of view [she said]. To learn one history or one literature, thoughtfully and well, does *not* mean opening one's mind to others. I need only recall, in the European system of education between World War I and World War II, the sustained emphasis in France—on the French language, French history, French literature and philosophy. All this did not notably deepen their sensitivity to things German. As for Germany, I do not think anyone will contend that the German of that generation, who steeped himself in German history, thereby came to understand the international spirit.

To the argument based on these rather extreme cases, Mrs. Birjandi insistently replied: "You simply cannot have an understanding of others before you have an understanding of yourself."

The controversy came to dominate the greater part of one particular day's discussion. In its course some of the broad exhortations on behalf of internationalism did not fare too well. Thus, for example, Rajkumari Kaur spoke rather drolly of more immediate problems in India: "I think we all, obviously, need to cultivate an international sense and sensitivity. But education in my country has some problems more urgent and concrete. I must, for example, first teach the children of the north of India to understand the children of the south, who speak quite different languages." Lakshmi Menon demurred that, nonetheless, any educational system obviously could encourage or stifle a sense of internationalism —simply by accenting either a concept of racial superiority or, at the other extreme, a consciousness of belonging, above all, to "the whole human family." While this was hardly disputable, the whole stress on internationalism came under brisk attack by Germaine Brée, perhaps conveying what disturbed some of the professional educators present (a small minority, be it remembered, of the conference).

We are using a term [Miss Brée confessed] that makes me, as a teacher, squirm. I cannot *teach* "internationalism." I can infuse my teaching with a certain spirit and sense of direction. Or I can teach international law—which *is* a discipline. But I think the most—if not the only thing—that can truly be done, as strict education, is to foster and to nourish the kind of intellectual courage that is capable of grappling with difficult issues when national self-interest is stirred and aroused.

Another American educator, President of Connecticut College Rosemary Park, offered an impressively outspoken assent to this caution upon the too self-conscious "internationalization" of education. "The fact is that all of us— from all parts of the world—have indeed had a good deal of what we are calling 'international education,'" she observed. "But we do not seem to have been able, by virtue of it, to influence significantly the trend of world events." Elaborating "an autobiographical illustration," Miss Park continued:

I was brought up in a time—between the two World Wars— when the air was full of talk of international understanding. All of us in scholastic circles were enthused about the League of Nations: We were committed to it, and it was the way to salvation. We all engaged in international congresses, exported exchange students, imported exchange professors, and multiplied our course in international relations as well as in the literatures and histories of other countries. Yet all this that followed 1918 did nothing to deter the coming of 1939. So I must raise the question: Was the fault with the quality of that "international education"—or were we simply trying to do something quite impossible?

There was, rather understandably, no swift and direct answer to the sweeping question. But the conference tacitly sensed and acknowledged its implications. For it clearly cautioned against grandiose, global generalizations about education, without reference to specific and attainable purposes. And it also quite as plainly cautioned against the inflated imagining of education itself as a cure for world sorrow or conflict.

It remained for a political philosopher, Hannah Arendt, to press the counsel of these cautions still further. "When we talk of 'teaching' attitudes—even benign attitudes like 'internationalism'—we risk confusing education with something quite different, namely *indoctrination*. I think it most doubtful if this is the task of the teacher." But Miss Arendt went on to question even the *efficacy* of attempting such "indoctrination." Observing wryly that there had been much talk of "objectivity" and "rationality," she tersely recalled a bit of ancient history:

Historical objectivity and impartiality may almost be called Greek "inventions." I suppose "impartiality" really first showed itself in our world when Homer decided to sing the praises not only of Achilles but also of Hector. In any case, there is no doubt that the Greeks were the first to discover and to use the astonishing human faculty of disinterested and dispassionate judgment. But—if we look upon the actual political life of the Greek city-states—we see that all this had not the slightest bearing upon the wars they waged, especially among themselves. These were frightful wars. They were wars of extermination—with the vanquished sold into slavery. And they were waged by a people who discovered, knew, and cherished the virtues of "impartiality" and "objectivity."

Under the force of such discussion there seemed to prevail, by the end of the conference, an unspoken acceptance of the fact that "the nation" and "nationalism" could not be consigned to the graveyard of history. It was not merely the logic of the discussions that fostered this tacit consensus. It was the compelling and obvious fact that the conference was being attended by representatives of so many newly born nations, just beginning to discover the trials and the dilemmas, the challenges and the excitements, of free nationhood. And could one seriously insist that the experience just beginning for them was, by some arbitrary fiat of the historical process, a mere indulgence in the obsolete?

Again, the outer world, with its infinite variety of institutional forms and popular purposes, echoed through the room and through the quiet, rambling discourse of two score women, considering the education of new generations.

The Dialogue between East and West

Perhaps no quality of the tone of the conference was more striking or refreshing than its freedom from the clichés and stereotypes so commonly afflicting exchanges between representatives of the Western and Eastern worlds. No Western conferee ever felt compelled to defend her society for its "materialism"; nor was any Eastern conferee provoked into apologizing for her economy's "inefficiency."

This mellow and mature note was struck, at the first session of the conference, by India's Lakshmi Menon. "What I most object to," she said bluntly, "is the tendency among us in the East to idolize the achievements of the West—or for you in the West to idolize some real or imagined values in the East." She went on:

I think it wholly wrong to contend that "spiritual values" persist only in the East and have simply disappeared from the West. The fundamental values of humanity, the universal values, are shared by the intelligent East *and* the intelligent West. A lust for wealth, or a passion for gadgets, or all the ugly and familiar signs of conspicuous consumption—these are not human failings confined to the West or to industrialized society: They can be seen in India too.

A little later in the conference, when some passing allusion was made to the record of Western urban society in terms of juvenile delinquency, broken families, and dubious general morality, it was Mrs. Menon who disposed of the implied indictment: "I do not believe that the West has more of these troubles—I think they merely keep better statistics."

In kindred spirit, the American educators took pains to make clear that they did not regard Western education—or Western society—as any marvelous repository of perfect answers to questions perplexing less advanced regions. The need to train specialized leadership—or an "elite"—for example, was obviously on the minds of conferees from Africa and Asia. But Laura Bornholdt quickly noted that the problem of an elite was far from being resolved in the Western nations: The *growth* of a scientific elite, effectively capable of deciding the destinies of their societies, posed dilemmas for which no Western educational system had devised answers.

Again, the problem of giving the individual a confident "sense of belonging" was posed, early in the conference, by the Nigerian lawyer and executive, Jaiyeola Aduke Moore —who had submitted, in a paper read to the conference, a graphic picture of the problems posed by the breakup of traditional tribal patterns and the sudden challenge of urban society. No Western educator rushed to assert that Western education had spendidly geared itself to the complexities of urban life. Rather did Rosemary Park observe with somewhat grim realism:

> The issue is to give the individual a sense of belonging in the community. I fear that, at the moment, in the most *advanced* countries, the whole sense of community has virtually broken down. The family structure, the religious structure, even the coherence of urban life itself—all have been shaken. If this is true, or largely true, we are not in a very good position to give instruction to the rest of the world.

Equally notable was the fact that such issues of political philosophy as did arise were never posed or argued on lines of West versus East. Thus, as already noted, the scrutiny of Indonesian "guided democracy" was pressed not by any Western conferees, testing the world by the tenets of Jeffersonian democracy, but by two inquisitive Indians. And the same conference session was enlivened by outspoken dissent on another issue: the danger (or lack thereof) of the encroaching power of the state in the sphere of education. A jurist from Denmark, clearly committed to the worth and wisdom of the welfare state, felt no worry about political authority. Unhappily and vigorously disagreeing was Margaret Ballinger, citing her long acquaintance with the educational system of South Africa—and the intrusion of state authority. As Mrs. Ballinger remarked to her Danish confrère, "Our experiences are simply worlds apart." What made the contrast interesting was that it divided conferees from two Western societies.

Only once—in the conference's last meeting—did a fairly deep difference of view appear along lines suggestive of East-West philosophic differences. Curiously, the dissent divided a Western ambassador to India, Sweden's Alva Myrdal, and Rajkumari Amrit Kaur, a member of the Indian Parliament. The conference had just reviewed some general conclusions on world educational needs, applauded by Alva Myrdal but with a renewed appeal to "rationality" to dispel the false images, propagandistic slogans, and gross simplifications of the Cold War. Indeed, with a quiet kind of fervor reminiscent of eighteenth-century rationalism, Mrs. Myrdal urged that the word "values" be stricken from the subject-title of the conference. The conference had, in fact, danced a most delicate minuet around the word "values" and (with the conspicuous exception of Elisabeth Schwarzhaupt's appeal to fixed "rights" and "absolutes") had dealt with "directions" in discreetly relativist terms. At this point Rajkumari Kaur broke in with the impatient air of a woman weary of verbal compromise:

I hear a lot of talk about *mental* development, but I have to confess greater concern with moral and spiritual development. I am quite aware that I am the only person here using these words, but—for me—they are the most important in the world.

When you speak of "rationality," I simply do not know what you mean. If, as I guess, it means complete divorce from religion, I can view it only as a sign of danger. . . .

Why must we shirk the words "moral" and "spiritual"? Without them—and what they stand for—what growth and development is there for man?

The rhetorical questions went, of course, unanswered.

The sovereign spirit of the East-West dialogue, however, remained throughout essentially the same: tolerant and comprehending. This spirit governed even at those times when discussion turned to differences in the two areas' historical evolution—particularly with regard to the slowly unfolding experience of democracy among the Eastern peoples, tremulously but courageously struggling to emulate Western example. And on this subject the most simple and poignant appeal came from Begum Ahmed of Pakistan. The gentle, almost touching rebuke to ideological purists of the Western democracies was spoken in these words:

I would like to recall that America's President Madison said that democracy, without an *educated* public, would be a farce or a tragedy.

Is it not creditable that there are newly emerging nations in the world, *without* the necessary degree of popular education, who have been able to establish the Western form of democracy?

At the same time, there are other young nations where the warning of President Madison still applies, where the perfected forms of Western democracy yet do not exist—yet where they are still clinging to the democratic *idea*. Here some freedoms can be fully allowed, others must await the wisdom of a public knowing how to use them.

Does this not deserve understanding? Should one not refrain from scorning a limited democracy as really not a democracy at all?

There are some of us nations truly democratic in spirit—and in the ideal we are working toward. If we have to follow some kind of "middle way," to avoid anarchy for a while, I think we deserve your tolerance and belief and encouragement. For, even if you do not accept and respect us as belonging, purely and completely, to the democratic world, you should know—and I assure you—that the ideals are within us.

Stirred by this spirit, the discourse between East and West could hardly fail to be mutually compassionate and sensitive.

The Role of the World Community

The conference achieved a consensus, emphatic and unqualified, on a number of injunctions addressed to the world at large and defining responsibilities in worldwide terms. These basic affirmations, reiterated often throughout the conference, were made explicit in the final session's summary by Rosemary Park. And they included the following:

First: With the fate of all peoples sealed in a common destiny—but with the gap between rich and poor, at the same time, becoming ever more deep and dangerous—the developed countries face a responsibility, far more urgent than they have realized, to give help to those less fortunate struggling to progress.

Second: Since education is vital to economic progress—and since it is, in fact, the kind of "investment" most availing for countries lacking in natural resources—any world programs of assistance must place vastly greater stress upon aid to education than they have done in the past.

Third: The key instruments and agencies for dispensing of such aid should be the United Nations and the worldwide voluntary organizations—for the aid should in no sense be used by the donor as an instrument of self-serving national policy.

Fourth: While the "importer" rather than the "exporter" of such aid to education should everywhere freely determine the substance and content of the education, varying with region and culture, yet there exists an obligation upon all, universally, to foster those values and attitudes sustaining a sense of commitment to "membership in the whole human family."

These were generalized conclusions. Behind them lay detailed discussion studded with examples of *both* the urgency of the need for action *and* the complexity of the problem of seriously meeting that need.

The evidence of the need for massive help came from all sides, and it was perhaps most striking in the case of the problem of literacy. There was the gently eloquent Aduke Moore to make clear that her native Nigeria, so newly born to the world of free nations, could not, in full reality, *be* a nation and *grow* as a nation without educational advance on the broadest front. There was Alva Myrdal's evidence (in her address to the conference) in historical terms: Over the past one hundred and fifty years the social and economic progress of even the most advanced Western countries could almost be traced and charted as direct coefficients of their educational systems. And perhaps most striking of all were the facts cited by the Argentinian economist, Elba Gomez del Rey de Kybal, on the problem of literacy in Latin America. As she noted, the Latin American continent's present population includes some 48 million adult illiterates. With a surging population growth expected to reach the mark of 320 million by 1980, Latin America gives warning that, at the present rate of school enrollment, the proportion of its adult illiterates will fall between *one fourth* and *one third* of all the people of its twenty republics.

Such sharp facts made the affirmation of the need for worldwide action more than a pious generalization.

Yet equally sharp were some of the problems and dilemmas apparent, from the discussions, in planning such action. Some pertinent and realistic matters were not even mentioned— such as the improbability of the American Congress' appropriating large sums to be dispensed by the United Nations for education in foreign countries, while liberally leaving the content of such education to be wholly determined by the distant beneficiaries of congressional largesse. But a number of other prickly questions were raised.

First: There was much concern expressed over political control by local governments exercised upon aid received from abroad or through the United Nations. With disarming candor, conferees from both the Far East and Latin America confessed their distrust of the disinterestedness, competence, or integrity of their own governments. And they indicated, at least inferentially, how much they would prefer some manner of neutral international administration.

Second: Despite the appreciative tributes to voluntary international organizations, there came lament from many quarters that these organizations sometimes seemed (from the point of view of the beneficiary of their help) quite disorganized themselves. At times they appeared uninformed of or indifferent to local and native assistance available for their well-intentioned programs. More often still, they seemed a little unaware of one another's existence and activity in the same region—or, perhaps, almost self-consciously competitive. The Korean educator Helen Kim murmured almost wistfully: "It is now eleven years since Korea began getting many kinds of aid, and we are grateful to all these different agencies of help—we welcome them all, we like them all. But—if they could just get together, we could all get along more quickly with the problems we face, and the people would have greater heart and hope."

Third: There was voiced even greater anxiety on the realistic question of whether financial assistance on a world scale did not threaten, almost inevitably, educational control. Laura Bornholdt stated the problem succinctly: "We seek, perhaps above all else, free thought, free communication, free inquiry. How do we guard such things, when the educational bills are paid by governments or official agencies of any kind? Will those who make such investment leave it free? In short, do we not have to hope to educate the investors, even before we start educating the young?" No one gave brisk answer to this riddle.

Fourth: There were many expressions of concern about the kind of education that could be "exported"—the kind of real assistance that could be extended, between nations and cultures, without "selling" one's own culture. A clear enough understanding emerged on a realistic distinction to be made between "training," in scientific and technological disciplines, and "education" in the broader sense. The former could be "packaged" and "shipped," while the latter could not. So far, so good—but Rosemary Park had a slightly disturbing question to pose to those countries aspiring to "import" such help. She asked:

We have seen in our own advanced countries that, by over-emphasis, "training" can gain too great an ascendancy within the educational system. This over-emphasis can allow it to usurp some of the place that should be taken by the philosophical or religious or aesthetic. We have had this problem. Can you—in the less economically advanced countries—feel sure of keeping "training" in its place, controlling this "export," and keeping your educational structure in healthy balance?

All of this pointed to the broad question: What should be the nature of the "commerce" in education to be expanded throughout the world community?

To this, some specific answers were formulated. They came, in general agreement, from the African and Asian conferees to whom the question was really addressed. And they were sharpened, too, by David Owen, executive chairman of the Technical Assistance Board of the United Nations.

It was agreed, for one thing, that the greater part of this commerce should be essentially "neutral" in content and technical. Its organization among nations should be, to the greatest extent possible, multilateral and apolitical. Thus, for example, a program subsidizing translations of technical books and publications would be of immeasurable value.

It was agreed further, and in much the same spirit, that it was crucially important for each nation to invest all available resources in developing its own educational structure—rather than that such funds be diverted into scholarship-and-fellowship programs providing study abroad for a select few.

Such philanthropic programs were, in fact, sternly questioned, particularly by David Owen, who scathingly alluded to competitive Soviet and Western scholarly forays in Africa as "body-snatching." And the consensus was that it was right and reasonable, especially in the newly emerging nations, that their youth find their education *in* their own environment.

And it was agreed, as a logical corollary, that each nation must staff its own educational system at the lower levels, particularly the primary level. This by no means precluded foreign assistance, foreign teachers, or studies abroad. But all of this should be concentrated in two spheres: first, the training of teachers, particularly for primary schools; and second, the more advanced or specialized studies, whether graduate work in the liberal arts or technical training.

Such were the few specific patterns of action discerned. They left much to be filled in.

Yet they plainly pointed toward some roads ahead, still uncharted and unmarked, urgently inviting the travel of minds fearless of the future.

The Role of Regions

There was no generalized conclusion to emerge more clearly in the consensus of the conference than the fact that no world-spanning generalization about education could be wholly valid. On the practical level: Each region had—and itself alone understood—its own problems. On the philosophic level: Nothing was more to be shunned than uniformity, nothing more to be respected than diversity. The *questions* about education more often than not were universal. The *answers* could only be regional.

There was humor—but there was also symbolism—in the laments expressed by some conferees over the failure of international agencies, in the field of technical assistance, to respect either local needs or local skills. Thus from Iran came the unhappy incident of five Iranian housing experts summoned by a United Nations agency to work on a distant housing project—quite soon after the agency had completed a like project *in* Iran without bothering to consult the same specialists. And from Egypt there came the understandable request that future shipments of clothing to needy females in the desert regions not include brassieres.

Analogously, the problems of education had to be met on their own distinct and peculiar terms in each region. Those of Latin America, for example, included some highly individual and indigenous matters. One such matter noted by the conference was the desirability of encouraging the repatriation of the many skilled Latin American professionals and technicians pursuing careers in the United States—by providing greater incentives and opportunities in the economies of their own countries. Such a problem hardly finds any parallel in Africa or Asia. Again, many a Latin American country finds a few professions (medicine, law, architecture) excessively popular and hopelessly overcrowded: the professionals are frustrated; their resources are wasted. Almost any African nation would welcome such a problem of specialized abundance.

Nor did it seem possible that any environment could generate so many unique problems as South Africa, so graphically reviewed by Margaret Ballinger. A nation of distinctly differing languages, cultures, religions, and races, it offers the singular spectacle of three million whites denying twelve million of other races any share in political or economic power. It is obviously a society divided against itself—and more than half of the African children attend no school at all. In such an environment, the most elemental propositions about education assume a strangely different cast. There is no more basic requisite, for example, than the teaching of language. Yet here language is a *weapon*—with the government insistent that neither English nor Afrikaan, but only the traditional Bantu, be taught the African population.

The fact is that, throughout the conference, there was hardly a major issue for discussion that did not rather quickly reflect regional distinctions and varying needs. Thus . . .

There was the weighing of the danger of state controls—particularly under the terms of "the welfare state." One session of the conference was largely dominated by the isssue after Begum Ahmed of Pakistan, addressing herself to the Western conferees, candidly asked whether the welfare state menaced individual or educational freedom—"*since we have no experience to judge by.*" With the confidence of one reared in Scandinavian political life, Alva Myrdal tried to respond assuringly that "a democracy, supported by educated and vigilant citizens, removes any such threat from the welfare state." But Rajkumari Amrit Kaur discerned the geographic and historic irrelevance of such assurance: "Your Scandinavian democracy has attained the degree of maturity and efficiency that gives *you* such safeguards. But there do not exist such checks on state authority in our newly emerging societies, where the majority are illiterate and look for a leader to follow. What do *we* do?"

No less vivid in revealing regional differences was the almost continuous discussion of the problem of *priorities* in educational needs: On which levels was most progress needed, most swiftly? At one juncture Alva Myrdal argued most plausibly that "the main efforts should be at the base and at the top." Specifically she called for stress on (1) training in reading and mathematics for the general population and (2) each nation's encouragement of some particular specialization, in the form of institutes of advanced learning, to endow each system with quality and pride. It followed from this that "what is really quite wrong is the over-emphasis on secondary education." This seemed quite persuasive—until Nigeria was heard from. As Jaiyeola Aduke Moore explained *her* country's needs: "In Africa, at least the part I come from, we have a certain amount of primary education. But when these children finish schooling, at the ages of eleven or twelve, we find them a floating population not really qualified to do anything—including getting employment. So the fact is that *we* need secondary education perhaps most of all."

As for the related issue of the education of an elite—of professional, governmental, and technical leadership—the wants and needs here, too, varied widely. Both Latin American and African voices were raised to recognize, often to emphasize, the need for their societies and economies to be spurred, by such leadership, toward the expansion that would broaden opportunity for all. Yet India's Lakshmi N. Menon sharply dismissed as alien to democracy such preoccupation with an elite's training. It is probably not unfair to say that the training of India's civil service and bureaucracy, already accomplished in decades past, allowed an Indian a luxury no African could afford.

The threads of diversity thus wove the pattern.

The pattern as a whole, however, was a plea.

It was a plea to men and women of all nations to summon their wits and their energies, their capacity for comprehending and their capacity for giving, to devise ways to allay the world's second greatest hunger—the hunger for knowledge.

Conference Papers

Editor's Note to Part II

The papers here published, nine in number, suggest the span of the conference's discussion—the range both of substance weighed and regions represented. Selected to convey this range and variety—with no disparagement to other papers equally representative—they have been edited to meet exigency of space and to avoid duplication of content.

Two papers from Africa come first. Aduke Moore reports on the social revolution in her native Nigeria, and Margaret Ballinger reports, with accent on education, on South Africa's struggle *against* change. Together the two offer a striking study in contrast—within the same continent in ferment.

From the Far East, from Pakistan and India respectively, come the modulated, questioning voices of Begum Anwar G. Ahmed and Rajkumari Amrit Kaur. Begum Ahmed tells—particularly through the wry musings of her young son—something of the mixed emotions with which the East views its own entry into the age of industrialization. And the voice from India closes its remarks, appropriately, with a recollection of the values of a Gandhi—and the prayerful hope that they not be "modernized" into oblivion.

The special problems of Latin America in the sphere of education recall the infinite diversity of the world's needs, and they are tersely set forth in the paper by Elba Gomez del Rey de Kybal.

Two papers look at the world through European eyes. Even as they complement one another, the accent in each falls in somewhat different places. From Germany, Elisabeth

Schwarzhaupt focuses on the division of the world and the values that Western civilization must strive to save in a mortal struggle. From Greece, Ketty A. Stassinopoulou perceives the forces of "communication" pulling the world together and envisions a *mosaic* of infinitely varied, yet basically harmonious, parts—a kind of "city of the world," recalling the Aristotelian vision, glimpsed from the height of purposes that must stir the whole family as one.

Finally, two citizens of the Middle East—Lebanon's Salwa C. Nassar and Iran's Parvin Birjandi—speak of the heart of the educational matter. For they talk of the individual, his hope and his capacity for growth, creativity, and dignity.

1. The Social Revolution in Nigeria

ADUKE MOORE

[NIGERIA]

The Heritage of the Past

T HE FAMILY is the center of the social and economic organization of life in Nigeria. To understand the present development of the country and its educational needs, it is essential to learn something of the structure of that organization, which existed in Nigeria and, indeed, in the greater part of West Africa before the advent of European influences.

The family consisted of husband and wife or wives with their children, commonly forming a close economic unit. But the word "family" was used in a much wider sense than that generally accepted in Europe: it consisted of a child, his father and mother, and his mother and father's brothers and sisters. The child would often refer to the latter as "fathers" and "mothers" instead of "uncles" and "aunts," and his cousins were regarded as his brothers and sisters. In a wider sense all members of the same generation within a group of relations or within a village group were regarded as relations who called each other "brothers" and "sisters." Because of these strong ties with the place of birth and the place in which the "extended" family lived, Africans, when they re-

35

ferred to their home, meant not the house in which they lived but their family's place of origin—even if they themselves were not born there.

There was therefore a strong sense of community, and the individual was educated by his family to realize his duties and responsibilities to his society.

To understand the social organization, the morals, the economic and religious concepts of a village or a clan, we must realize that the concept of the community embraced not only the living but also the dead and the future generations. The land never belonged to an individual and could not be alienated, for it was handed down by the ancestors who were considered the real owners, the present holders being trustees who had to transmit it undamaged to the future generation. The whole existence from birth to death was considered in a series of associations.

The individual's need was subject to that of the community, and his life had value only within those close ties of the clan. There was a well-established line between persons who commanded and those who obeyed. In spite of this there was a notable absence of class distinction as is known in the Western world. This was due in part to the organizations of age grades: education was through this age grade, with the result that people of the same age group went through similar experiences and thereby developed mutual respect for each other's talents. The acceptance of the leadership of the most capable followed naturally from this, while enabling the community to recognize the value of each person's particular talent and to afford it a place in the community's scheme of things.

Thus the Nigerian community was a tightly integrated one. From childhood to manhood, every phase of the individual's and the community's life was ordered and defined. And each member had his duties to perform and his responsibilities to bear—in childhood, in adolescence, and in adulthood.

Though there was no "book" education in the old society, the form of education given was suited to the needs of the community, and this is still the case in many places in Africa today. Many men and women who have never been to school, or in contact with Europeans, show such tactful and dignified behavior—and so much wisdom and refinement —that they are, in the broader sense of the word, well educated. The education of young children was left very much in the hands of the women in the community. It was characterized by its leniency. The child was often left alone with his playmates and was expected to find his place gradually among his own age group. At other times he followed his mother and assisted her in whatever work she was doing. Thus in the simple circumstance of clan or tribal life in which he grew up, attended by the kindness and thoughtfulness of relatives and not hampered by social disabilities, he learned that the ultimate aim of each child was to serve the community. Under such education a "spoiled" child was a rare thing. Emphasis was laid on proper behavior and respect toward elders. The games played were often imitations of adult activities, and in this way children grew up accustomed to genuine work. The girls' formal and more serious education began at an earlier age than that of the boys, for the mothers needed their help sooner.

During adolescence the serious and intense education began, often through initiation rites. Both boys and girls passed through this. The most important task of the woman in the life of the clan was considered to be childbearing. For this she was prepared as a girl by receiving instructions from the older women, often her own mother, about sexual and maternal life, her conduct toward her future husband, her duty generally as a housewife, and any special customs of her clan or tribe. While the boy was being given an intense physical education, he was also brought into close contact with the past history of the clan, which had been handed down by his ancestors, and with the beliefs and customs which were the keys to it.

The vital idea in all this education was that the existence of the clan depended on the perpetuation of this inheritance. Both boys and girls were taught to become willing members of the community and to learn to serve the clan. Self-control, reverence for the old, the interest of the clan—these were the supreme criteria. The boy gained in his turn—not only by learning tribal customs and taboos, farming methods and traditional crafts, but also by feeling himself a well-protected and valued member of the clan, properly possessing pride and dignity.

All these traditional patterns were related to and reflected in the economy of Nigeria. It was mainly a subsistence economy, and to a great extent this is still true today. The man, his wife, and his child each had his or her own part to play in tilling the land to feed the family. Often by the age of ten or fourteen the child was given a small piece of land on which to cultivate his own crops as his contribution to the family stores. He might also learn the art of weaving or basketmaking in the off season. The wife also helped on the farm and grew the crops for the family's daily food, leaving her husband to deal with the heavier chores of the farm. Seldom did the family unit consist only of a man and wife with their children. More often a man had many wives— often a sign of wealth—and it was the duty of each one to till her own piece of ground and to contribute to the feeding of her husband and children.

The chief or head of the tribe had the land vested in him as trustee, and he saw to it that each family was given a piece of land to farm. Unless the family died out, this land would not be taken from them. They were not allowed to sell it or part with it in any way, as it was given to them to farm for the benefit of the continuing family. Land, to the African, was not a valuable object to be exchanged for other things: It was the resting place of his ancestors and the inheritance of his children. So the clan was, and still is, averse to selling any of its land. This has meant continuity of ownership but also considerable inflexibility in dealing with land—a rigidity that has perhaps contributed to slowing the economic development of the country. For foreign firms are rarely anxious to invest large sums of money for development of a land on which they do not have complete ownership or at least a long lease.

The Impact of the New

The European invasion of Africa was not the first invasion, and it would be inaccurate to say that Africa had lived in complete isolation before its modern contact with Europe. In early times merchants from the north and east came to Africa, and some even settled here. But their social, cultural, political, and economic influence could reach the interior of Africa only in very thin streams, with so many interruptions as to leave sufficient time for the people to assimilate what was congenial to them and to reject what was not. The new culture then enriched and stimulated the traditional life and did not necessarily cause a breaking away from the old. In fact, the foreign immigrants were assimilated and became part of the tribe or clan.

The invasion of the European at the end of the last century, however, was of a completely different nature. Whereas the traders of olden days came in small numbers and were assimilated, the Europeans came in much larger numbers and at closer intervals. They were not, at that time, interested in the customs and the culture of the countries: they conquered or colonized and claimed the right to preserve intact their own civilization. This often meant forcing their own customs on the African, and to a large extent they succeeded in doing so. Governments, the missionaries, and the economic activities of the European—these could be said to be the three forces responsible for the disintegration of Africa, its culture, and its social customs.

The shock of the impact of these forces can be quickly seen in three instances: the effect of urban life on family responsibility, the role of religion, and industry's employment of women.

1. Whereas in the village community and family, education is total—with all aspects learned together slowly— education in the urban environment is split, fragmented. For more than half of the working day the child is undergoing formal education, which is only a part of his requirement for adjustment to changes in his environment. If his father works till the late afternoon, and if his mother helps provide the means for his education by going to the market to sell till the evening, the child leaving school at two o'clock may be completely without guidance or restraint for a third of the working day. When his parents return in the evening, they may be too tired or too full of other interests to provide the complementary instructions so characteristic of the village family. If the child is a girl, she may be required after school to join the mother in the marketplace to assist her. In a way this is an extension of her education, but it does not provide as much as the rural family, in fitting education to the needs of the child. This is not a plea for children to be retained in the rural environment but merely a statement of the problem. Although boys' and girls' clubs are now increasing and give valuable training in the art of living together, one cannot escape the feeling that something is still missing.

2. It is well known that Africans have a strong affinity for religious organization, and for many women, religious or-

ganizations constitute the most important outlet for self-expression, as well as a means for acquiring a measure of confidence in dealing with unfamiliar situations in modern living. In traditional society, sex, age, and experience determined precedence, and it is difficult for the old people to imagine situations where competence and a different kind of experience is required, irrespective of age or sex. This leads to conflict between mother and child, husband and wife. This conflict has led to strained family relations and to the breakup of the family life. Many homes are saved only because of the religious beliefs of the wife and the satisfaction she gets from taking part in religious organizations. It is often represented that Africans have no taste for voluntary social organization. This impression is created because they are more interested in their immediate family clan or tribe. But it is in religious organization that their capacity for voluntary social organization can best be seen. There are also excellent examples in the group contributions that in many cases have provided the means for the university education of one of their family or clan. Today Africans are gradually taking over work in such societies as the Red Cross, the Blind Society, leprosy relief associations, and other organizations designed to help women in particular. The women as well as the men are also active in community development and to some extent in mass education. As more and more women become educated and acquire the confidence essential to play their part outside the traditional framework, while at the same time keeping the dignity of their past, so will they be able to take on more of these responsibilities.

3. Now that "economic development" is constantly on the lips of governments, and technological changes in rural agriculture are under way, one major problem is the provision of something to occupy and absorb the energies of women in the rural areas who constitute so large a part of the agricultural work force. As this prolonged process of techno-

logical change proceeds, the position of women is bound to be ever more deeply affected. The growth of rural schools, for example, removes from their mothers the full-time care of children of school age. This is a problem which the community-development planners and administrators will have to examine very carefully. The transformation of society to meet its changing environment calls for education in the most wide and deep sense. There is, moreover, evidence that —particularly with regard to attitudes toward non-group members—women are more conservative than men. In Nigeria, for example, the crossing of group lines, through intermarriage, has been resisted more by the older women than by their menfolk. But as education spreads in Nigeria—and especially as higher education is acquired outside the immediate reach of the group, where pressure can be organized—the tribal hold will be less.

Meanwhile, in the urban areas women are now working in offices, stores, and factories as well as following their more traditional occupation of trading on their own account. They are able by these means to continue to contribute to the education and well-being of their family; in fact, in many instances it has been the mother whose trading has allowed her to send her child for further education abroad or at home. But there are not nearly enough jobs in the towns for the young men and women who wish to work after they have left school. They are no longer interested in the land, and they unfortunately are not qualified to take jobs requiring special skills. This is a pressing social problem, and further education is, of course, part of the answer.

The Role of Education

For all the urge toward industrialization, some 75 per cent of the adult labor force of Nigeria still is engaged in agriculture, forestry, and animal husbandry—with cultivation of the fields and tree crops providing at least 50 per cent of the national income. After agriculture, the related service industries account for the largest male employment—including such occupations as drivers, stewards, other domestic workers, dock workers, miners, and quarry workers. The reason for the large number employed in service industries is probably due to the production of cash crops, both for home and foreign markets, by thousands of small peasants —requiring a vast marketing organization. The distribution of consumer goods on which, with the introduction of money economy, the peasant spends his surplus cash, necessitates a system that can speedily take these goods to the market village. With this clear paramountcy of farming and trading activities in Nigeria, industry is not yet a major contributing factor to the national income—even though, as in most developing countries, the word "industrialization" is a magic one.

With the realization that Nigeria's economy is of this nature, it is apparent that one of the main problems is the intensified education of the people looking toward greater improvement in farming methods. This, in turn, can quicken the pace of industrialization. None of this itself, of course, will solve the problem of the disintegration of both the old tradition and the security of the clan or tribe. This, I feel, can *only* be achieved through education in the broadest sense.

Modern education was first brought to Africa mainly by the missionaries. To be able to teach the Gospel to the people, they had to introduce, as a matter of expediency, a certain restricted amount of learning. The object, however, was to produce clergy to preach the Gospel and win adherents: It was not a planned education system to meet the needs of the people. Rather, somewhat the contrary: In most instances it was designed for the destruction of the traditional culture of the people. And this to a large extent has caused the African to develop an inferiority complex about his own traditions—without having acquired anything substantial to replace them.

Later, government and commercial enterprises took an interest in the education of the Africans, but again this education was geared to meet specific needs (clerks, interpreters, bookkeepers, etc.), and there was no systematic modern education devised to serve the community. All education thus was toward the introduction of an alien religion and an alien commerce. It had an unsettling effect on the old society, as the whole tendency was to despise and ignore the culture of the people and to give preference to the alien one. The result was that the young people tended to leave farming to become clerks in simple imitation of their European masters.

An educator who approaches the civilization of a country with respect will take care that that civilization is incorporated in the education of the children and that they are trained to respect and love it. For the fundamental objective of education in modern times is to enable a community to comprehend, and even anticipate, changes in its environment and to make the necessary adjustment in order to survive in it. The concepts of the good citizen, the just man, the devoted parent—all are fundamentally concerned with the survival of communities or societies. But in periods of rapid environmental changes these qualities are clearly not enough. The basic requirement that education must strive to provide is the ability to *think*—or perhaps even better to *perceive*—in the sense that one should be able to see valid relationships between things and events which appear unconnected. Unfortunately modern Western education in Africa did little to serve these values. Always it was heavily weighed with various presentations of the European image. French-speaking Africans or English-speaking Africans were subjected to an intense process of absorbing the records of triumphs, the heroics and history, of their respective metropolitan "mother countries." Until recent times (the school books *are* somewhat better now) nothing was taught about the civilization of Egypt, Samaria, China, or Latin America. The effect of this was to destroy the African's respect for his past, the belief in his abilities, and therefore confidence in himself.

Interdependence among peoples and cultures requires, perhaps first and foremost, self-respect and self-confidence. Education in Africa therefore has the special task of restoring these vitally essential qualities. And the future of education will therefore involve a complete revision of curriculums and teaching techniques devised by Africans for themselves.

In all economic and social development, the improvement of the *human* material—its competence and efficiency in making the most of the community resources—is the supreme and first task. In Western European countries, where education is rather taken for granted, tremendous emphasis has been placed on *material* capital assets. Hence, until recently, the cry was for more and more capital for developing countries. The recovery of Germany, however, after the virtually total destruction of her material capital assets, has demonstrated that the true essentials are human—knowledge and skill and self-confidence.

In the African traditional system the rich man was under obligation to give freely to assist the poorer members of his family or his clan or even his tribe. This, combined with the fierce search for knowledge, meant that a great deal of his resources went into financing the education of his family or tribe, directly and indirectly, through group contributions. Thus was financed a great deal of primary education which the state could not until recent times provide.

Today the crucial importance of education in the development of Nigeria is not being neglected. This is amply demonstrated by the Commission on Post-Secondary and Higher

Education, set up under the chairmanship of Sir Eric Ashby. The commission's report has recently been published. Here briefly are some of its recommendations:

1. Nigerian education should for ten years or so become an international enterprise, since there is a great shortage of qualified teachers. A loan and education aid program should be set up on an international basis so that young teachers from all over the world will come to Nigeria on short contract to man the classrooms.

2. There is most urgent need for more secondary schools, so that the number entering secondary school will be increased threefold. National high schools should be established all over the federation, and they should begin as sixth forms, the lower classes to be added as teachers become available. Eight training colleges are needed to give a two-year course leading to Grade I certificates enabling the holder to teach in primary schools.

3. The technical institutes existing are far too small. They should be expanded so that at least twenty-five hundred young people a year can be qualified as technicians.

4. The agricultural institutes should be on the same level and scale as the technical institutes.

5. There are two universities in Nigeria. Two more should be built right away. One of these should be for people who are already in jobs and have, through lack of opportunity, been unable to study before. Classes would be held in the evenings, and degrees would also be offered to people who are prepared to take university courses by correspondence.

The Nature of Our Interdependent World

Behind the feeling of national independence is the idea of mutual respect on the international level. This rests on the record of heroic achievements of all nations, whether in the field of art or of science or of philosophy or even of war. It is true that today the history of Africa is being gradually and literally unearthed and brought to light. But this is not enough. The generations of Africans from now on must be able to add an increasing measure of their own to the stream of international achievements. This means that they must be able confidently to take from the world pool of knowledge and achievements—and add to it with their own contribution.

This relationship requires a number of conditions. First, there must be a measure of freedom from "the European image." Secondly, there must be acceptance of international definitions of standards *but not* of *form*. For all peoples must have freedom to produce things, or to make contributions, that can be seen to be distinctly their own. Perhaps the field of art is the best illustration. Africans must continue to produce works of art that are distinctly their own—conforming to international standards of quality, naturally reflecting the trends of an age, but nevertheless giving clear resistance to the temptation to fall in with the ideas of other nations and peoples about *form*—in short, the temptation to *imitate*. They cannot hope to establish claims to lasting achievement on such blind imitation of other nations.

The key to successful living in an interdependent world is understanding—and sincere appreciation—built on deliberate education. The process should no longer be left to the operation of chance forces and decisions. Up to the 1950's it was the rest of the world that was obliged to adjust itself to Western Europe and North America. Since then it has become the task of Europe and North America to adjust themselves to the rest of the world.

One illustration will suffice to show the kind of adjustment necessary. For many years Western governments represented to their people the great sacrifices that they were making in order to help the peoples of the underdeveloped countries. Until the last year or two the sacrifices that the peoples of these underdeveloped countries made, though not consciously, in order to assist the peoples of the developed countries were ignored or concealed—except for a number of critics regarded often as cranks of one sort or another. Now that the people of the developed countries are being asked to make greater and greater sacrifices to assist developing countries, it is difficult to justify the size of aid by pointing to the benefits they had received from these developing countries—without substantial revision of the picture as it had been painted in the past.

This does not mean that people of the developing countries are not appreciative of the aid given to them. It merely means that full recognition of what they had themselves done before would make acceptance of such aid more honorable and dignified. Even more, it means that the peoples of the more developed countries must not be tempted to regard peoples of developing countries as inferiors or "country cousins." Such temptations—and misunderstandings—would hardly have arisen had the doors of education been fully opened to their less fortunate brothers, and if they themselves had been *educated* to appreciate the contributions of the developing countries. In short, a serious sense of equality is absolutely essential for international living today.

Finally, I believe that one of the most important requirements—for any nation to participate fully and confidently in the world community—is a restored and renewed appreciation of one's *own* past and hence a belief in one's ability to produce at standards internationally accepted and respected.

Clearly this means for Africans a certain amount of reorientation toward their own history. There is at present in Nigeria one group, the Historical Society, which has this formally as its aim. It is a good beginning. Another group, the Contemporary Society, is mainly concerned with examining the wider international scene. The International Women's Society is aiming at a better understanding of each country's social problems. These societies illustrate the ways in which the problems can be met.

Beyond this, our leaders—not merely the most prominent ones, but everyone to whom others look for guidance in matters beyond their experience—need to develop a kind of "sociological imagination." They must learn to be able to stand back from their immediate environment and to appreciate and encourage the process of change as it unfolds.

To this process, we are, in our day, committed. It remains to us to see that it proves, not destructive, but creative.

2. The Seething Division in South Africa

MARGARET BALLINGER

[SOUTH AFRICA]

T O LIVE ANYWHERE IN AFRICA is not only to be conscious of a changing world; it is to be in the very midst of it. To live in South Africa, as I do, is not only to be in the midst of change but to be met every day with the problems and the challenges that the new world emerging around us throws up. It is also to be the immediate victims of the almost frenzied tempo of change which leaves little opportunity to achieve something of the perspective and the emotional detachment that are the essential conditions of reasoned judgment and the only safe guides to reasonable adjustment.

South Africa is a microcosm of the world as we know it. Here we have in a domestic form every relationship and every situation that today challenge the mind and the spirit in the dangerous field of international affairs. South Africa has two white groups, with considerable affinities, it is true, but with a background of difference and even of conflict rising at times to open war, leaving its own train of highly emotional memories. It has different languages, different religions, different levels of culture, and it has different races and colors. In addition it has different economic levels which have tended and which still tend to follow the lines of other dif-

ferences, aggravating their divisive force. Above all, it has a
strongly entrenched tradition of privilege which lends peculiar significance to all the other differences. All political
power and all economic power rest in the hands of a small
section of the population: some three million whites who
have consistently refused to share it with the twelve million
who differ from them in racial character.

Thus we have haves and have-nots, rulers and ruled, imperialists and subject peoples, in a world that is committed
more and more against these differences of condition and
status and any system that seeks to maintain them. Privilege
is everywhere being challenged, mainly because those who
have been its victims are no longer prepared to continue to
accept their inferior position, while those who have enjoyed it
are committed by their own profession against it and cannot
therefore resist the challenge.

But it is one thing to concede the right of all men to share
the good things of this world and the power by which they
are sustained; it is another to insure that they shall do so. It
is one thing to subscribe to a declaration of human rights;
it is another thing to discover how the rights which that
declaration enshrines shall in fact and in practice become a
universal heritage.

The majority of white South Africans believe that in the
circumstance of today this objective is beyond our capacity to
achieve. They are firmly convinced that the concession of
political rights to their own non-white populations must inevitably mean the destruction of all the standards that give
Western civilization its form and its content and make it
worth preserving. They argue that, on both the political and
the economic fronts, these standards, if they came to rest in
the hands of our at present unenfranchised majority, would
crash—due to the ignorance and incapacity of people who
have had too little experience of their working and have too
little understanding of the principles and the practices that

uphold them. In support of their argument in this regard, they point to the happenings around us both in Africa generally and in our own community—and not without effect.

The weak link in their argument is, I believe, the time factor. Not all white South Africans believe in the superiority of the white race or share the view that the challenge of destiny to the white man in Africa is to help to maintain a white community. Not all by any means would endorse the terms of Dr. Malan's letter to an American correspondent about the moral foundation of apartheid, suggesting that there is a basic and essential difference between black and white that makes it impossible for them to live peaceably together. A great majority, however, would find themselves in sympathy with the argument that it will take generations before Africans can come to understand both the political and the technological techniques upon which the modern states of the West have been built, and can be trusted to sustain them. Such an argument, in practice, comes very close to the "superior race" attitude.

That South Africans should tend to fall into these attitudes is at least understandable. What is more alarming in this modern world is the ease with which other groups, who are not faced with the peculiar challenge of our society, under the slightest provocation manifest the same prejudices as those South Africans are guilty of so often. I do not mean merely to refer Americans to their own domestic situation. We have witnessed the same kind of thing quite recently in England. And I have just been in Australia, where I was staggered to discover the ease with which color prejudice has raised its head there.

This situation is fraught with the gravest danger to the peace of the world. Emerging nations, so highly and understandably sensitive about race attitude, are also for the most part economically insecure, which naturally aggravates their sensitivity. For those of us who believe that personal freedom is the essential condition of the good life, it is important that the balance of power in the modern world should be in our favor. As yet, most of these emerging nations are uncommitted. We must do what we can to insure that eventually they support our conception of the principles upon which society should be based.

Surely this is where education must and can play its part— and that a major part. It is not enough to hand out material assistance to emerging communities, to help them toward improved economic development and rising standards of living. The people must be helped to *use* such assistance to their best advantage. And this means applying the experience of the older, industrialized states who have long since discovered the crucial advantage of a rising standard of education for all their people.

There can be some differences of opinion as to where the emphasis in such education should be laid. On the basis of my experience in South Africa, I still tend to favor emphasis on the conquest of illiteracy—at both the child and the adult levels—as the beginning of the process of "leveling up." And thereafter must come a drive to provide the technical education vital in modern industrial society. I am inclined to place less stress on the immediate need of university education, not because I think it is unimportant, but because in my own experience university education has been looked after with greater sympathy than any other section of our educational need. And in this connection I would remind you of the action under the Colombo Plan which has already resulted in the establishment in Melbourne of an international house where, in fact, students of all colors are being brought together at the university level.

Inevitably, the emphasis I would place in education rises out of my own experience with South Africans. The situation we face here is that at least 50 per cent of our African children are still not in school, even though we are a highly developed industrial community. We have practically no technical training for Africans at all. The great gap in this regard is particularly noticeable in the field of agriculture. It is not surprising that we have no such technical education, for the simple reason that color bars prevent South Africans from using technical skills. The whole of our agriculture is based on Africans who are obviously extremely inefficient, and I have wondered for many years why we have not applied ourselves to the problem of raising our agricultural level, which is an obvious problem for every emerging country.

The situation in South Africa has turned up some other points worth noting. For one thing, it has raised the question of language for emerging nations. This question has arisen, in special form, by virtue of the stress that our government is laying on language in the vernacular—which means neither English nor Afrikaan, the official languages, but the Bantu language. The government has been insistent that this should be the medium of instruction for our African population on the ground that it is part of their inheritance. But, significantly, our African population is resisting this pressure to the utmost on the ground the Bantu language is going to isolate them from Western culture and slow their development.

Another critical issue, though less peculiar to South Africa, is the necessity for improving the status of teachers—if whatever education given is going to be of any real worth. A teacher must be able to live at a level worthy of the community's respect, if he or she is to have significant effect on the intellectual growth of that community.

All these are problems of education for the sake of material advance; but the sum of them is almost a relatively simple issue when compared with the *political* aspects of our educational needs. For the *values* on which the free society, as we understand it, must be based are much more difficult to teach and to learn: tolerance of differences of opinion, government by discussion and persuasion rather than by authority and compulsion. We can relate economic and technical progress to these political values only by noting that a rising standard of living can help to remove some sources of abrasive attitudes in personal and political relationships.

Beyond this, respect for personality—and for the principles upon which democratic practices are based—must, I believe, be demonstrated and stimulated by the more highly organized communities who have themselves been responsible for the developments, both political and economic, that have changed the character and the condition of the world in this last half-century.

These advanced communities, I submit, have an immediate concern of their own. The changing world faces them with a domestic problem, as well as an international one, and a problem that is fundamental. This is the problem of maintaining the quality of personal freedom within managed economies and despite the widening area of governmental activities contingent upon the development of the welfare state. In these days—particularly when they are days of full employment and rising standards of living, as they have been in many of the older industrialized countries—we have to be reminded, and to remind ourselves, that the price of freedom is eternal vigilance. I am particularly conscious of this because the liberal principle—and I use the word "liberal" as simply showing recognition of human values— has been a slow plant in South Africa; and it is showing all signs, even now, of being smothered by the activities of a government with very rigid ideas of its own.

In these circumstances there are grounds for believing that while the emphasis on education in new and underdeveloped countries will inevitably be on the technical side, there is a need among the older states for a new emphasis on the "liberal" side, a renewed emphasis on the cultural against the vocational in education. This, of course, is easier to say than to practice. People must still, quite clearly, work to live, and education has inevitably become largely vocational. And my own views are probably colored by the conditions in my own country, where government exercises an ever tightening control over education, and there are great pressures on every level to give education a specific stamp.

Under such pressures the maintenance and spread of human values has, it seems to me, become increasingly the function of organizations *outside* the classroom; and I believe that it will probably have to go on being so, at least with us. There are a number of institutions and organizations that are trying to fit themselves into this gap and to fill it. Among them are organizations of students, especially with international affiliation, special activities of universities not allowed now under our law to be multiracial, and parent organizations working in the area of race relations. Groups like these are doing their best to keep alive the sense of human values which our educational system is often denied a specific right to maintain.

In short, we need everywhere, I believe, to renew the individual's sense of his own responsibility to himself and to his community. This imposes, I feel strongly, particular obligation on the *advanced* society, for it is vital—for *all* societies—that there be retained and enhanced the quality of those societies that claim to be free and pride themselves on their freedom.

Only thus can we create a true sense of the greater community of all humankind. Only thus can we show a positive and dynamic faith in the destiny of our civilization—about which I have no doubt—and this destiny is surely to show that all people, no matter what their differences of race, color, or creed, can live together in peace, harmony, and mutual respect.

3. The Quest for
the Whole Man

BEGUM ANWAR G. AHMED

[PAKISTAN]

I‍T HAS BEEN SAID by a famous poet of my country that the meaning and purpose of education is to enable man to live a good life. Education, according to him, is a dynamic process which must sustain, as well as challenge, knowledge.

The question is: What is the good life? The prophets and the philosophers in the past have defined it in moral terms. Several of them, however, accepted as part of the order of nature the poverty, hunger, and disease that have been the lot of man.

Modern times are characterized by a determined effort to understand the forces of nature in order to control them and use them to serve man's purposes. The accelerating process of science and technology has opened up vast possibilities for good or evil. But if the right choice is made—and, indeed, it must be made if humanity is to survive—the elimination of hunger and disease from all the world has now become a practical proposition, rather than a visionary's dream. The people everywhere are awakening to the expectation that poverty and ignorance can be banished from the face of the earth, and that it can happen soon—in their own lifetimes.

Today all countries in the world, whatever their state of

57

development, are endeavoring to move ahead with all possible speed. Powerful political and psychological pressures are building up behind man's insistence on a better life. This is true in developed as well as underdeveloped countries. Everywhere it is understood that social and economic development depends on the acquisition of knowledge and skills, which are the products of education and which alone provide the base for the determination of social patterns and economic growth. In the developed countries education has adapted itself to the need of producing the requisite knowledge and skills. The underdeveloped countries must build upon the same foundation. With so little done and so much to do, this is in some ways our most difficult problem. We are just beginning to teach our teachers.

Industrialization has everywhere brought great, and sometimes bitter, social changes. This was true of the Industrial Revolution in the land of its birth. This is true of Russia and China in our own time. The social changes are inevitable. The bitter price is not. The newly emerging nations must hope, through wise education, to smooth the transition and avoid the loss of human dignity and human freedom.

Economically developed and underdeveloped countries must work together to meet the challenge of our time—that all humanity be freed from hunger, disease, poverty, ignorance, and subservience. Some developed nations have responded admirably to this challenge and have offered technical and financial assistance generously to liberate the people of the backward countries from crushing social and economic disabilities. But the full significance of this new type of international cooperation is still insufficiently recognized. Some developed countries give little, some give grudgingly, some hold fast to the vested interests of another century. At the same time many receiving nations show a lack of appreciation and, sometimes, even apprehension. Ancient fears and hostilities are not easily forgotten, and the sins of other times and places are visited upon a guiltless generation.

Education must stimulate universal awareness of the interdependence of all economic and social groups, and of all nations, in this modern world. The cult of nationalism must progressively give way to internationalism. Nothing that happens in one country today is without meaning for the rest of us. We have all become part of each other, in the practical sense of survival. In this fast-changing pattern of values, education must not only solve problems of the present but anticipate the problems of the future.

I would like to digress here a little. I feel that one of the problems most urgently before us is the complex and subtle matter of the *spirit* that must underlie true mutual cooperation. The manner can matter as much as the substance, when aid between nations is given and received. This aid must be given with sympathy, with respect, and with understanding—not as a coin to a beggar. And I feel that here both the developed and the underdeveloped countries have to make a greater effort to know and to understand each other's problems.

I should like to tell you a little story that might help make clear what I mean. Not so long ago, I saw my son scribbling something on a piece of paper, and I asked him what he was doing. He said there was a debate in his college, and the subject of the debate was: Is the influx of Western culture harmful to the youth of Pakistan? When I asked him if he were supporting or opposing the proposition, he replied, "It all depends on how many points of arguments I can collect for either side." I asked him, "How many points have you got in favor of the motion that it is harmful for Pakistani youth?" And he answered, "Well, if I speak for the motion, then I shall talk of things like broken homes, juvenile delinquency, the unwed mothers, the homes for the aged, the alcoholics—and so on." And on the other side of the argument? "Oh, I intend to speak of democracy as a form of government, and I will speak about freedom of association, equality of opportunity, social security, the status of women, and I shall then go on to talk finally of the welfare state."

I said to my son: "The things you mentioned first, in case somebody refers to them, are as alien to Western culture as they are to ours. They are the by-products of technology. And the other things are what Western culture really stand for." But I said to myself: I wonder how many other young people in Pakistan have this conception of Western culture? And how many young people in the West have any idea of our culture? My son at least knows that behind the ugly things on the Western scene there are the finer ideals. Do the people in the West know that behind the flies, behind the dust, behind the tattered clothes of the East, we are a people also with a deep culture and a sense of values? Do they know of the patient woman who, having become a widow at the age of twenty-five, would never marry again, because she feels that her duty is now to her children? Do they know of the young man who, from the age of eighteen, begins to earn his living and continues till he is an old man, but does not marry—because his duty is to enable his sisters to marry and to make his mother comfortable, before he begins to enjoy life himself?

Such values fill our culture. And every culture has its own serious values. All must be appreciated and sympathetically understood—if there is to be world cooperation of true meaning. And at the same time—in this revolutionary age we live in—we have to guard these precious values through all the great changes brought by industrialization.

Industrialization inevitably brings stress and strain. In the underdeveloped countries, industrial labor must be drawn mostly from the rural population, and adjustment is difficult in urban surroundings. The exacting disciplines of factory work are unknown to a rural community. To make adjustment easy and to prevent economic waste, it is imperative that extension work in rural communities be so devised as to inculcate the higher disciplines of performance.

Again, industrialization brings many changes in the structure of the family. Communities living under the joint or extended family system lead a sheltered existence: the individual is not exposed to the need and urgency of incurring direct responsibilities and making unassisted decisions until after attaining maturity of experience under corporate guidance. In the industrial society, based on the nuclear family system, young people have to find a home immediately after marriage and to face the exacting problems of modern living. Education must be so designed as to have the maximum relevance to these, the practical problems.

I look back on our society in the past, for example, and recall how the daughter-in-law, newly coming to the husband's family, continued, as it were, to enjoy being a young woman—with the mother-in-law, or whoever was in charge of the family, bearing all the responsibility. Yet it had been instilled in us from birth to learn to be obedient wives, to be good mothers, to make sacrifices for the family, so that even when we married very young, we had a kind of maturity. Today it all seems different. Today the responsibility for the family does fall on the young married girl. Yet today we are so busy trying to educate her for so many things in this fast-changing world that we have not given much thought to preparing her psychologically for the responsibilities and sacrifices and adjustments of marriage.

Thus today—while most underdeveloped countries are straining to achieve a quicker economic growth and a higher standard of living—there is, at the same time, increased skepticism about the degree of happiness which material progress can bring. There is a fear that industrialization, with its corollary of urbanization, will inevitably produce an exclusively technological culture which will undermine spiritual and moral values.

Material progress relieves man from the struggle for the

satisfaction of his basic needs of food, clothing, and shelter. This is all to the good, but it is at the same time necessary that the greater physical and mental leisure, which comes from freedom from this elemental struggle, is used to best advantage. Therefore, it is necessary that man's intellectual and spiritual growth keep pace with his material progress, so that he is enabled to develop those values that will insure the good and the happiness of humanity.

Here we must go back to the prophets and the philosophers. It must be the function of education to inform the heart and spirit as well as the mind of man; to produce the skilled man, the cultivated man, the free man, the good man—indeed, the whole man.

4. The Quest for the Healthy Man

RAJKUARI AMRIT KAUR

[INDIA]

W E LIVE in a dynamic world that has changed almost beyond recognition within the last decade. Whole continents have awakened from an age-long slumber, as it were. New values and new outlooks have emerged, and continue to emerge, by reason of this awakening, and also because of the amazing scientific discoveries which have conquered old geographical barriers and have made the world into what it is today—a really small place.

It is a tragedy too deep for tears that even while all of us want peace and are convinced that war offers no solution to any problem, we still live under the shadow of conflict. The greatest thing, therefore, that challenges us is to educate ourselves to banish from our hearts that psychology of fear which gives birth to mistrust and suspicion, and which, in turn, prompts us to arm ourselves with weapons of war in order to avoid war. Surely this is an absolute contradiction in terms. Moreover, this shadow throws one of the biggest obstacles in the way of economic development for the under-developed countries, as well as hinders the social advancement of all the countries of the world.

Americans live in a country that has resources in abundant measure; I come from a country struggling to give a bare minimum to its people. India has, however, a background of thousands of years of an ancient culture and civilization, which still dominate the lives of our masses. How long they will continue to do so—with the enormous impact that Western civilization has made and continues to make on the Orient—is difficult to foresee.

At the same time I have no doubt in my mind that while we have an enormous amount to learn from the West, there are many things that perhaps the West may learn from us. The teaching of history in every country has never given a fair picture to the learner's mind. Invariably there has been a tendency to place a point of view before the child that whatever his government or his country did was right. We have therefore—all of us—to unlearn a great deal of what we were taught.

How can we educate ourselves to know each other better in a world where every corner of the globe has become easily accessible to all of us? Efforts should be made, I think, to allow a more free and far greater interchange of youth, whether as students or as helpers in the social services. If international good will is to be built as it should be, it can be done only through this type of interchange among the young—who are much more likely than we of the older generation to rise above the man-made barriers of caste, creed, and race. Children are never inhibited by these barriers. Why we grow up to erect them is something that we must ask ourselves.

I have said that the teaching of history has rarely been on proper lines, but I also believe that education in its entirety has to be reoriented to meet the great challenges of life in today's world.

This certainly needs to be done in my own country, and I wonder whether the same is not required everywhere. Is not the academic side being neglected in favor of the administrative, with less and less contact between the teacher and the taught? In what we call a scientific age, is not too much stress being laid on the sciences and too little on the humanities?

We have everywhere to face the problems of juvenile delinquency and youth indiscipline and, further afield, of general mental ill health. What are the causes of these disturbances and afflictions—except that we have ceased, as did our forefathers, to lay great enough emphasis on the moral and spiritual values of life? Educators everywhere have to consider how best to turn the thoughts of mankind away, always, from things temporal toward things eternal.

The West has realized that we cannot afford to live in a world of haves and have-nots. And those of us who come from the East, where economic development has not been possible owing to circumstances beyond our control, are grateful for the help that we are today receiving in every sphere. And this help must continue in as great measure as possible, and always with no strings attached, because everyone has a right to put his own house in order in the way he thinks best. But I would like here to draw attention to the fact that while economic development is being stressed all the time as the be-all and the end-all of the accepted goal of prosperity, little emphasis is laid, nationally or internationally, on the development of the human being.

There can be no true happiness, in my opinion, if the health of the community is below par and if the members of that community are not educated. Millions of children on the great continents of Asia and Africa, and even further afield where primitive tribes still exist, do not have any opportunities of education. Likewise, millions do not have enough to eat. Medical aid and relief not being available, all kinds of disease ravage these lands; environmental hygiene and sanitation are nonexistent; a protected water supply is not available; and until and unless such subhuman living conditions are improved, there can be no economic or social development in the true sense of the term. If we want our children to learn, they must have healthy bodies and minds. If we want our farms and industrial labor to produce, they must have skills and, therefore, the education to acquire those skills. In a scientific age the youth of every country must have opportunities to acquire technological education. Frustration, born of lack of opportunities to learn and to serve, must be avoided at all costs, if we are to preserve the principles of a democratic way of life.

I would therefore like us, who are assembled here, to raise our voices in support of much more money being made available, both nationally and internationally, for the social services.

We in India, as also in some other countries of the East, are suffering from the problem of overpopulation. This is something that has to be faced and yet is very difficult to deal with. Tradition and custom die hard everywhere, particularly in a country where the women are uneducated. In addition to our poverty, we have outmoded social customs to overcome. For example, ours is a land of universal marriage and, alas, very early marriage. The responsibilities of parenthood are, as it were, thrust on our youth, regardless of whether the prospective father is a wage earner or the prospective mother is mature for childbearing. In spite of what the government is trying to do, no measure for family planning can bear any visible fruit for at least a generation or so. I have always been of the opinion that in addition to any chemical or mechanical devices that may be resorted to, the greater benefit will accrue from educating our men and women to agree to raise the marriage age of their sons and daughters, while also educating the youth of our country to refuse to marry until and unless they are competent, materially and morally, to undertake the responsibility of the procreation of children.

Asia, Africa, and (nearer home to you here) Latin America

today present a formidable challenge to the Western Hemisphere. I am glad that President Kennedy has promulgated the idea of what is known as a Peace Corps, composed of young persons (but, I hope, not too young) who have the urge to serve those less fortunate than themselves. If those who join it are of the right caliber and properly trained—and these are big "ifs"—its work should yield dividends.

I would prefer, however, to see such a force working under the aegis of an international voluntary organization, rather than under governmental auspices. Further, I would prefer such a corps to be an international, rather than a national, one. More than once, from public platforms, I have for some time past advocated an international force of persons qualified to work for health and education, the members of which would be willing to go to any part of the globe to render service. And if any such organization could work under the sponsorship of a body like the International Red Cross, I believe it would be received with open arms everywhere, and no ulterior political motives would be ascribed to it. It may well be that racial antagonisms and prejudices may be reduced, if not eliminated, and violence arrested by an unarmed peace corps, if the same could be led to work in the way advocated by Gandhi.

After all, it is only through serving each other that we can hope to win over even those who may be bitterly opposed to our way of life. And those who are in the glorious position of being able to share their talents through service must be at all times perceptive and willing to learn. My own experience has taught me that some of the wisest lessons that I have received came from those whom I, in my folly, at first thought were ignorant. Nor must the recipients of help be oversensitive. Today they receive. Tomorrow they will give.

We may not—indeed, we must not—simply fear communism or totalitarianism. We have to turn the searchlight inward. We have to ask ourselves how best the democratic way of life—with its freedoms of speech, thought, and action—can be proved, in and by our own lives, superior.

The *via media,* between the extreme right and extreme left, has to be followed. While the state has to be responsible to a large extent for the welfare of the people committed to its charge, it must in no wise arrogate to itself the power to eliminate voluntary endeavor. For voluntary endeavor carries within it the moral and spiritual urge to serve humanity in need. And this can never be replaced by governmental machinery, which by its very nature has to be soulless.

In this materialistic age I want the spirit of man, the divine spark in him, to be free to give and to create. I would therefore plead for money being made available by the United Nations with no strings attached, through voluntary international organizations such as the League of Red Cross Societies and the International Conference of Social Work. These groups, through their national society members, can help voluntary endeavor in the countries concerned.

In any event, to keep alive the flame of voluntary endeavor is to my mind a duty that devolves for the greater part on my sex. Are we women prepared to take up so great a challenge today? If we can meet it, it will certainly be the biggest contribution that we can make toward world peace.

In the ultimate analysis, if we pursue the right path and work for it, we should be able to move as rapidly as possible toward a world government. With that, all of the sums today spent on armament could be utilized for the uplift, both material and moral, of the humanity whose need for help we can neglect only at our peril.

In conclusion, I would like to quote what one of the great thinkers of today, Arnold Toynbee, said to an American audience recently, for it finds a deep echo in my heart. "Gandhi's techniques," he said, "answer precisely the needs of mankind in the atomic age. His spirit will continue to work in the world. Gandhi was not purely an Hindu in inspiration; he also drew on Christianity. In this sense, we may see the working together of these two great religious traditions, as mankind faces his crisis."

Have any of us the faith and courage to follow these techniques?

5. The Economics
   of Education

ELBA GOMEZ del REY de KYBAL

[ARGENTINA]

T HE CONCERN of this paper is the interrelation of education and economic development. More specifically I am concerned with the educational needs of the Latin American countries in their struggle for economic growth—and with the responsibility that the national and international communities have in assisting this economic struggle and meeting these educational needs.

It is assumed that what is uppermost in the minds of the citizens of the underdeveloped countries today is the need to accelerate economic and social development. By this is mainly meant an increase of the standard of living of the population, not merely by raising the national income but also by its better distribution.

It is also assumed that, with a few exceptions, the Latin American countries have already passed the "take-off" stage of their economic growth. What most of them need is rapid action of a magnitude sufficient to give intensity and acceleration to that process.

The intensive research upon economic development in Latin America, carried out during the last twelve years, particularly by international organizations (the United Nations,

70

the Organization of American States, the World Bank, etc.), permits us to draw a number of conclusions. These include also an evaluation of the role of education and training in accelerating economic development.

From the standpoint of economic development, three factors are of basic importance: natural resources, physical capital, and human resources. It has been demonstrated that in the present stage of technology, *natural* resources are *not* the determining factor in economic development: Countries like Switzerland, Holland, Denmark, and Norway have achieved a high level of development despite most meager endowment in such resources. And experience has proven that investment, though more directly related to economic development than to natural resources, varies greatly in its effectiveness. Venezuela is a good example of large investments and lagging development. The problem is not only to bring about an increase in the share of the national product devoted to investment as opposed to consumption; it is also to bring about a more desirable allocation of investment. And to make a full use of capital investment, a qualified managerial, engineering, and labor force is necessary for the selection, operation, and maintenance of such investment. Thus the human element is not only the *aim* of economic activity but the most important *factor* in determining the level and composition of the underlying investment. It follows, then, that education and training are of primary importance not only from the subjective point of view of the individuals receiving such benefits but also from the standpoint of accelerating the economic growth of a nation or of a region. No investment is more productive than that in education and training.

A few facts and figures can suffice to illustrate the implications of this—and the magnitude of the educational problem—in Latin America. The basic fact is that 15 million Latin American children—that is about half of the school-age population—lack schools. There are 48 million adult illiterates. The total population of the twenty Latin American republics is about 190 million, and, since it is growing faster than any other major area of the world, it is expected to reach the 320 million mark in 1980. Under these circumstances all indices of growth must keep abreast of this population explosion of nearly 3 per cent per year. Thus, although primary and secondary enrollment in Latin America increased 48 per cent between 1948 and 1957, the bulk of this increase was absorbed by the population increase. During this period of time the school enrollment ratio increased from 30.2 to only 35.9.

Unless school enrollment in Latin America can be dramatically speeded up during our generation, it is likely that the region would reach the turn of the century with perhaps a third or a fourth of its adult population illiterate. It is also sad to note that school enrollment has grown at a slower pace than industrial production. This gap is all the more serious since industrialization must necessarily provide the principal impetus to economic growth in Latin America. The most hopeful institutional event of recent years—the signing of the Montevideo Treaty envisaging the creation of a Latin American Free Trade Area—will be greatly handicapped if shortages of skilled personnel emerge as the main bottleneck to the industrialization of the region. Brazil, for instance, foresees a 20 per cent deficit in industrial technicians, and at present its industrial schools are supplying only about 45 per cent of the country's demand for skilled workers.

What remedies can be suggested for preventing at least the worst consequences of Latin America's lag in education and training?

The first question is whether the major part of the effort in this direction should come from inside the countries concerned or from the outside, through multilateral or bilateral aid. Any realistic analysis of the question leads to the conclusion that in nearly every instance the bulk of the effort must come from the country's own resources. For that purpose a painful reform must be undertaken over a period of years in the fiscal field to increase public revenues and particularly to change the pattern of expenditure, cutting down on such items as military appropriations and all types of ostentatious projects and activities, in favor of education and public health.

Another essential reform, even more important than the fiscal one, is a revision of the existing educational curriculums at all levels, adapting them to the needs of growing economies. A reorientation and a modernization of existing institutions could be enough in certain cases. For instance, there are some careers—like medicine, law, dentistry, accounting, architecture—that commonly attract the largest numbers of the youth of the underdeveloped countries. The number of graduates in these areas simply exceeds what their country can economically absorb, and there result two kinds of problems: frustrated technicians and a waste of scarce resources.

Beyond this, some countries stand in need of complete revision of their educational system as a whole—unifying its technical and social aspects, and democratizing its whole structure.

The Committee of Twenty-one of the Organization of American States, in its meeting at Bogotà, Colombia, in September of 1960 summed up the *international* aspect of this problem as follows:

It is in this necessary and urgent transformation of concepts and systems that the possibility that international action will supplement beneficially the efforts each country is making in the framework of its own definitions appears most clearly. The problems that might be taken into consideration are related to the needs for financing, both economic and technical; in the teaching order, to the improvement of teaching methods, particularly with a view to supplementing the necessary and inevitable presence of teacher and textbooks with the more efficient use of modern methods for the communication and dissemination of ideas. The tasks that teachers and professors should perform have to keep pace with every phase of educational demand. The absence of modern materials and techniques limits to an extraordinary extent, however, the productive capacity of teachers. Here is where broad perspectives open up for inter-American cooperation.

In view of the shortage of means, both financial and human, several questions of method and procedure must be faced. What strategy should be used to advance education in Latin America?

Here are a few general but relevant thoughts:

1. To what extent should educational resources be used to create a technical elite rather than to reduce illiteracy? I believe that in a number of countries there is a point beyond which economic progress would be stimulated more by training truly competent technicians—particularly in education, public administration, and enterprise management—than in using the same resources to reduce further the existing illiteracy. I also believe that unless a minimum core of technical personnel has been created, no effective consciousness of economic backwardness can arise—and no effective means to combat it can even exist.

2. Is it more advantageous for the Latin American countries to send people for training to the United States or Europe, or to have professors from abroad teach students locally? With certain exceptions arising from geographic proximity or type of training, I believe that in most instances an equal investment will be more productive if used to bring in, for instance, three foreign professors to teach economics at a South American university than if used to send fifteen South American students to study abroad.

3. What is the relationship between the training of technical personnel and local demand for their services? Nor-

mally this question is seldom examined, and in actual practice there is no way to obtain a precise answer. The fact is that many Latin Americans who have received costly technical training abroad cannot find a suitable occupation in their home countries. Many of them remain in the country where they receive this specialized training—particularly the United States. Others come to the United States to use the technical knowledge already acquired in their own country. There are thousands of Latin American professionals who have immigrated into the United States. "Operation repatriation" of professionals could be started by providing incentives for their return to their home countries—giving them opportunities comparable to the ones that are available to them in the United States.

4. At what level should people from Latin America go to study abroad? Again, in general terms, it seems that the best results are achieved with people who are already firmly rooted in their own countries, who hold some moderately responsible position, and who go abroad to specialize in an activity they are reasonably certain to continue upon their return. A particular group that should be given priority consists of university professors, who should be sent abroad in large numbers, then to return to disseminate their new knowledge. Incidentally, a much greater effort must be made by the universities in Latin America to have a full-time faculty, instead of the part-time professors who have to depend on outside employment to make a living.

5. To what extent is national sovereignty hampering the extension of technical knowledge in Latin America? It is paradoxical that nearly all Latin American countries have legislation protecting the local market for a number of professional occupations, particularly medicine, even where the ratio of doctors to population numbers is very low. There is no regional system for accrediting colleges in Latin America and for an automatic validation of degrees. These are ob-

stacles that the future Latin American Free Trade Area will have to tackle.

6. What would be the single most effective use of Public Law 480 funds in the field of education? There is a shortage in Latin America of modern textbooks in Spanish or Portuguese, as well as of other reference material. A much larger number of technical books—especially of college textbooks—should be translated and published at subsidized prices as a matter of first priority.

In brief, if the national and international communities do not take bold and concerted action in the field of education to correlate the educational facilities with the need for economic development, the gap between industrialized countries and underdeveloped countries will continue to increase. There is no greater urgency than taking action to reduce *the gap in knowledge*—since this quickly translates into an even greater gap in production and income.

The crucial responsibilities here are *both* national *and* international. And education has a vital role to play in *both* the most developed *and* the least developed nations.

In the underdeveloped areas the national communities themselves have all too frequently failed to make necessary efforts to accelerate economic development. Institutions and practices that are deterrents to growth are still too prevalent, and the environment is not sufficiently favorable to encourage growth. And a paramount factor in this indispensable change in environment is the broadening of the educational system and its better adaptation to the needs of the economies in process of development. This is a *national* responsibility.

On the *international* level, multilateral and bilateral aid programs have not attained the desired impact. The reasons have been many. Usually insufficient resources have been used. Often the fields to which the limited resources are applied have been too numerous. And the methods and criteria for selection of projects have not been the most wise and effective. This situation is true in every area where an evaluation of international or bilateral foreign aid has been made—including the educational field. What is now urgently needed is a revision of the scope and the methods of these programs.

And all this points to an *educational* problem within the *most* economically developed nations. For they have generally been too slow to see the problems of the underdeveloped countries in all their magnitude. One reason for the inadequacy of multilateral and bilateral foreign aid has been the lack of knowledge of the situation they sought to correct. Here rises a tremendous responsibility for leaders in the educational field of the industrialized countries, and especially of the countries providing foreign aid. The success of their programs will depend, in great part, on their knowledge of the underdeveloped countries. And this knowledge can be acquired only through a system of education that teaches about other cultures and other nations, their problems and their languages, with far greater intensity—and insight—than have been shown to date.

6. Conscience and Coexistence

ELISABETH SCHWARZHAUPT

[GERMANY]

I T IS ONE of the basic facts of human life that we grow up and develop in isolation and differentiation from others, on the one hand, and in a state of social intercourse and give-and-take, on the other. Our approach to the stranger, to other kinds of people, is at once negative and positive. Both these elements are necessary for the individual to develop a personality.

This interplay of contrasts also exists between nations—more sharply and more overtly. In this field, besides mutual acceptance or rejection as between individual nations, there is the relationship between large groups of nations governed and directed by various regimes and different ideologies. Here we have the problem with regard to that ambiguous word "coexistence."

Today there is a tendency in the Western world toward greater flexibility of outlook—no longer to consider the nation as such to the exclusion of all else, but to be more conscious of the larger communities of nations. This is true both on a continental scale and in terms of the world community as a whole. Today our acceptance of others is not without enthusiasm.

This tendency springs from economic, political and humane, pragmatic and ideological sources. Such fusion of rational and emotional motives in political movements brings with it both opportunities and dangers. The opportunities arise from the stirring and strengthening of political and ethical forces among large and powerful sectors of the people. Thus, at the present time throughout the entire Western world, religious, ecclesiastic, and charitable motives are contributing to provide help for the nonindustrialized peoples of Asia and Africa—and that is a good thing. With regard to my own country, which at one time received so much help from others, I can only say that all its ethical forces should be at work to support the efforts to assist the developing countries. The more powerful and charitable these forces become, in relation to economic interests, the sooner an indispensable prerequisite in this area will be established—namely, the unselfishness that respects the idiosyncrasies of others and their way of life, and hence does not presume, insist, or insinuate that our kind of existence (or our attitude to work, or death, or the opposite sex, or the state) is the only right one.

The danger in all this, on the other hand, is that the effects of any mistakes made are multiplied in proportion to the international implications of the political decisions to be taken.

A most particular risk is involved in the situation between the Communist and the non-Communist countries. In the leading political circles on both sides, the readiness to establish contacts—to be accessible for exchanges on both cultural and economic levels—springs from totally different motives. And a particularly striking example of this is to be seen in sharply different constructions put on the word "coexistence."

As a technical expression of contemporary politics, the word and the notion are taken from the dictionary of communism. According to Leninist doctrine, the word denotes a passing phase in the era preceding the attainment of Communist world rule. For the Communists, a state of peaceful coexistence signifies certain restrictions on the means used to arrive at the spread of Communist principles. But it does not mean the slightest relaxation in the *aim* of communism—for the Communists, the most perfect state of society—which is to achieve sole world domination. This is one of the obligatory dogmas proclaimed in every Communist school and during training in all industrial enterprises.

In the West the term "coexistence" has a different ideological background. Here it is applied by a society where tolerance—the readiness to acknowledge other social and political forms—prevails. Whereas communism—regardless of the form of coexistence prevailing at the time—stipulates absolutely the standards of its social system to be applied both within its own country and in all other countries, the West is increasingly willing to give simply *relative* values to the standards governing its system. This means, however, that, in our relations with the Communist power bloc, we are in danger of losing the healthy equilibrium between acceptance and rejection of other national peculiarities.

This problem takes on a certain urgency among the younger generation in the Western world, who have acquired a classical education in secondary schools. Their view of the world—discerning (contemporaneously) the diversity of nations born of a variety of civilizations, and (retrospectively) the succession of historical eras and their myriad changes—enables them to see good and evil, nefarious and enlightened forms of government existing simultaneously or consecutively. These young scholars are aware that forms of government vary among the nations according to the history, stage of development, and character of the peoples concerned. They rightly realize that the Anglo-Saxon form of Western democracy cannot be prescribed for all peoples at all times.

Moreover, they also come to perceive that dark ages of cruel tyranny often witness outstanding achievements in, for instance, the fields of art and science. And this further en-

courages us in the West to exercise that laudable attitude
of tolerance, for the sake of the freedom of the individual,
even toward such political systems as do not modify their
use of power as much as we consider necessary.

If I may refer briefly to recent history in Central Europe,
it is a mistake to believe that totalitarian systems with all
their abuse of power, such as national socialism and communism, have been supported only by uncouth, uneducated,
or half-educated individuals like Hitler. Among those who
were blinded by such systems we time and again have found
individuals with a first-rate academic education.

The clearer all this is to the educated classes in a nation,
and the more extensive those circles are in a nation, the
greater is the danger that the ethical standard by which our
policies are guided in the Western world will disappear. For
these policies, a necessary criterion must be maintained—
namely, the extent to which power is exercised for the sake
of the individual, his freedom, and his welfare. It is by that
criterion that we gauge the right of the governing authorities
of the state to tamper with freedom or to demand sacrifices.
It is necessary everywhere for the state to put limits on
freedom and demand sacrifice for the common weal. But
the essential matter is whether or not this power is wielded
with respect and consideration for man's freedom.

The paradoxical truth, then, is this: The more wholeheartedly we care about and "accept" the individual who
lives under a different regime from ours, the more decidedly
must we condemn and "reject" any state system that disregards that individual's freedom and privacy.

The experience we have had, in the history of the times
through which we have lived, compels us to seek permanent
basic values. It is my own firm conviction that such guiding
lines, such mainstays, can be found only in the realization of
the link between our earthly existence and a transcendent
world of common and absolute commandments imposed on

us. The guarantee against the abuse of state power is to be found in a law to which the holders of that state power are also subject. The law can fulfill this function of impartiality only if, in itself, it contains an absolute standard. Both a positivist legal doctrine and the historical and psychological relatively of nineteenth-century legal philosophy lead us into regions where we lose our way.

It seems to me that only the Christian basis of our civilization—of which many of us are not consciously aware but which is nevertheless common to most of us—has enabled us so far to maintain a sound balance between acceptance and rejection of other national traditions, creeds, cultures, and state systems. In this spirit and with this foundation, the idea of world community can be freed from illusion. In this spirit we can calmly face the disillusion that often afflicts all idealists working in international organizations, such as UNESCO and the United Nations, and the organizations of European cooperation. The conscience that rules them—and us—has to have two aspects. It has to respect all citizens of different history, culture, and forms of government. At the same time it has to uphold the special standard of the rights of all peoples to live in liberty under the rule of absolute law.

I would appreciate your understanding why I have stressed these two aspects of international cooperation. I came from a nation of whose people one third is living under the rule of communism, two thirds under the rule of Western democratic principles. We have to face, with special urgency, the problems of a community of men living under different forms of government and different ideologies.

7. Communication and Education

KETTY A. STASSINOPOULOU

[GREECE]

Our century—this turbulent, anxious, too often tragic and cruel century, yet so full of adventure and creative imagination—has been christened with many names. Because it has been so evidently many-sided, the names have varied vividly: the atomic century, the century of welfare, the century of man, the century of the machine, and so on. Frequently we have heard it called the century of communications. And I should like to review some aspects of this concept of our age.

Communication is not only a practical way of intercourse and exchange, important and vast in its achievement and implications. It is also and primarily a means of acquiring intellectual knowledge, and it can lead to understanding of the heart between individuals and groups. In *Adventures of Ideas* Alfred North Whitehead sees relations between human beings oscillating between "force and persuasion," and he adds that "the worth of men consists in their liability to persuasion." Their dependence on force, on the contrary, can destroy civilization. Now who could fail to see that, as communication has diversified and intensified contacts among men, it has at the same time opened the routes for free persuasion for men from different regions, of different races, and of different occupations?

Is not free persuasion the core of the philosophy and the purpose of the United Nations? "The creation of the world," said Plato, "is the victory of persuasion over force." Could we hope that with the tremendous development of communications there might come the creation of a new world?

The implication for education is, I believe, rather transparent. But notwithstanding its self-evidence, I think it must once more be stressed. Knowledge has too often been poured into the heads of the students, sometimes even imposed on them. The teacher in our day must use quite new methods. He must take the trouble to *communicate*—to explain, vividly illustrate, and earnestly persuade. We cannot instruct young people by the old signposts used by traditional education. We have to come nearer to them, rely mainly on discussion —and truly *communicate*.

It is, I believe, evident that in our day humanity is facing needs and problems, in the cultural and political and social spheres, in quite a different way from that of a few decades ago. Even that quite recent period was stifled in provincialism. Now winds, coming from the four points of the horizon, have opened wide the shutters that once closed the world from our view. The era of the parochial has sunk into the past. This is now the ecumenical era. And our interest is now plunging into the unknown, the unseen, the unexplored.

How does the teacher, then, make persuasive knowledge available to groups and individuals? My belief is that the scene we must use, the range of examples we should have at our command, the images we should try to make vivid— all must be drawn from the *whole* world. We must strive to widen students' horizons, ecumenically, as much as possible. We must help youth not only to become alert and cognizant of knowledge on as universal a scale as is humanly possible, but also (and much more difficult) to be sensitive to feelings in their different shades in all the world. To achieve this, the educator must possess openness, flexibility, and vision.

Can we deny that if our curiosity of mind, our vision of the world and humanity, have taken this ecumenical route, this is certainly due to the extension of communication— not only physical and material communication, but also communication of ideas and feelings and faiths? Can we possibly minimize the effect upon our lives of the facilities of travel, of meeting, of taking and receiving messages, of mass media of every sort, of exploring land, sea, and sky? Can we not see what all this means for us, as we try to know, understand, and interpret human beings and the different situations in which they are involved? And our understanding need not be in parts and fractions: It can be as a whole. For it is an undeniable fact that if we truly want to know anything, we must learn to see it whole—not necessarily in all its minutiae, but in its main lines and character.

As individuals and groups—educational groups especially —we have the obligation to help those whom we have accepted to guide to become aware and to understand this ecumenical aspect of our era and the significance of communication in it. This is the challenge. We shall have to provide ways and means to meet it. We shall, I believe, have to seek information, to find new ways of learning, to stimulate our imagination, and to use it to the utmost.

Imagination is without doubt one of the more powerful means with which nature has endowed man for broadening and deepening his vision of the world, and curiosity is one of the springboards of imagination. The educator must, in our changing times, take advantage of this source of fresh and ardent desire in the young for knowledge. Allow me to go some millenniums back, to recall our old historian Herodo-

tus, who, in order to write the history of his own country for
the benefit of his fellow men, thought he had first the obligation to traverse the world. Arriving at Memphis in ancient
Egypt and consulting the all-powerful and all-knowing
priests of Egypt, he asked if one of them could give him an
explanation of the river Nile's floods. The Egyptian priest,
surprised, had no explanation to offer. The curious and imag-
inative Greek traveler offered two or three. He was looked
upon with pity by the official custodian of static knowledge,
who said to his eager visitor, "Oh, you Greeks! Will you always remain children!" Precisely this "childlike," eager thirst
for an explanation is what educators have the duty to develop, in order to tap the vivid and powerful sources of
imagination.

Today's trend of life and thought, and astounding technological progress, are helping us in this direction. In the
eighteenth century the whole of Paris was looking aghast at
an Asiatic man and for months stood wondering, "How can
one be a Persian?" Even for people of my generation certain
large areas of the world remained, till lately, largely myth-
ical: The citizen of China was always a round-headed man-
darin with a long plait, always smiling with a sophisticated
courtesy; and all Arabs could be imagined only as riding
endlessly on camels in the desert. Now communication has
largely banished such fancies. The remote and the imagined
have become near and real. And hence the feeling of involvement, of belonging, has grown and passed from the tribal
group, the city, the state, the national frame—to a sense of
the universal. I do not mean by this that frontiers have
broken down or that we must put aside national loyalties.
On the contrary, I want to stress that, through becoming acquainted with the different aspects of humanity, we can now
study and better understand *differences* as well as similarities the world over, and accept and respect them. As a great
philosopher of our times has said, "The fundamental purpose

of communication is to enable men to agree . . . if only to agree to differ." Is not this a fundamental aim of our times?

I think we have in recent years rather excessively stressed similarities, which is easy and even a bit naive, and we have tried to build on these our efforts to sustain world fellowship. But the acceptance of *differences* the world over—this is a goal of worth to us as educators. In November 1959 the fourteenth United Nations General Assembly adopted unanimously the Declaration of the Rights of the Child. Its first principle runs thus: "All children, without exception whatsoever, shall be entitled to their rights, without distinction or discrimination on account of race, colour, sex, language, religion, political or other opinion, national or social origin, property, birth or other status, whether of himself or of his family." This principle—of fully accepting differences from earliest childhood on—is at least proclaimed by all responsible people, even though it is unfortunately not universally applied. For acceptance of differences demands courage. It suggests attitudes that might even be deemed revolutionary. It most surely requires a pioneering spirit.

Now pioneering has always had a great tradition in this country, and it is natural, I am sure, for anyone born in the land of Ulysses also to consider it a most precious quality. For pioneering means adventure, and it has been said that "without adventure, civilisation is in full decay." The educator therefore is challenged to excite the spirit of adventure, of exploration, as a means toward knowledge. How is this begun? By accepting as one of the axioms of our times the fact of its ever changing—by considering, as a key to our interpretation of the world, the old and so wonderfully modern saying of Heraclitus: "You cannot step twice into the same rivers, for fresh waters are ever flowing in upon you." This condemnation of intellectual conformity, of traditional repetition, contains the key to the educational process needed by our changing times. This does not mean the uprooting of all permanence, mere aimless and meaningless adventure. Rather does it mean an awareness of values of permanence, by discernment of the myriad forms and expressions they assume.

There may be those who fear that broadened communications can cramp or even kill the spirit of adventure; that the unknown shrinks at every new stride of communication, be it in the physical sphere or the sphere of the mind; that therefore adventure cannot have the romantic appeal of bygone years; and that everything nowadays tends to be predictable, tabulated, taken care of. This seems to me a shortsighted view. I do not think that any century has compared to our own in opening new horizons for adventure. For all our advances in communications, I would hesitate to believe that the spirit of adventure that lured Columbus to American shores was very different in quality from the one that now calls man to and beyond the stratosphere. Both expected to establish "communication" and to enrich fabulously humanity's heritage in knowledge and other goods. Both expected to meet differences. Yet I wonder if we are now emotionally more prepared to accept them than were the sailors of the *Santa María*.

Keeping in mind all these aspects of communication, we clearly see that it is a primary function of the art of governing. The roads of communication must be kept free and broad and open—and as diverse and enticing as possible. They must be kept clean of superstitions, shadows, misunderstandings, and fears.

Nowhere can this ideal picture be made so actual as in a college or university—a place of observation and knowledge and experiment where communication and cooperation are the basic instruments of learning. Such a college can also be a perfect field for the experience of meeting, accepting, and respecting individual differences, and thereby developing individual personalities for the ultimate good of each one and of all. In such an atmosphere can be found all the necessary flexibility, adaptability, and insight that Epictetus believed essential to human understanding. As this Stoic philosopher professed: "It is not the things themselves that upset and trouble men, but their dogmatic beliefs about them." We can, I feel sure, transpose these wise words and conclude that quite often when trouble occurs, it is caused not so much by the human beings themselves as by what is thought or believed about them by other human beings. It is often enough asserted that learning needs only an observant eye and an attentive ear, and this view is perhaps generally accepted; but I do not feel overoptimistic about it myself. For Heraclitus emphatically warned: "Eyes and ears are bad witnesses to men if they have souls that understand *not* their language."

The greatest foe we have to fight if we want to achieve understanding is, I believe, rigidity. One shudders when thinking of the terrible mistakes that are due to inflexibility, to conviction of infallibility, to the absolutism of monolithic minds. Such minds cannot see either shades or combinations of colors. They are, to my thinking, the most dangerous elements in a society or group. It is a gross delusion to call them stable or, as is sometimes done, to give them the halo of the idealist. Rigidity is not, to my knowledge, a component of faith. It may be taken for evidence of immaturity of thought or debility of feeling. The precious worker in cooperative effort is the receptive one who is forever developing. And, by necessity, developing means adaptation, communication, interchange, enlargement.

The other frightful danger of our times is standardization: producing people who all go the same way, indifferent or oblivious or even hostile to differences. We can observe clearly around us this deadly standardization advancing from "the field of the washing machine to the field of the mind." This would imply leveling, and we all know that leveling is a downward process, toward lower ground. Mowing a lawn gives us a picture of this process. All sprouts are cut off, all those fragrant wild flowers and spry herbs are leveled, and the lawn takes on the dull uniformity of a carpet. Every particularity, every precious individual difference, had vanished. Yet, with human beings, it is the differences—the uniqueness—of personality that we must strive to preserve. This is an imperative, a *must*, if we really want to escape the shaping of man's society into the deadly form of a herd without a soul.

There are, and we know it, important and even basic differences between human beings, their faiths, their social cultures, their political philosophies, their intellectual development, their economic levels. If—while keeping our own—we fail to recognize these differences in others, if we fail to make the effort to understand them and respect them, the whole edifice of our civilization will be in grievous danger.

Some may object or express a fear that accepting and respecting differences might well serve understanding, but that it will prevent cohesion and unity, that it will be the end of the different disciplines—social, moral, and intellectual—and will, step by step, lead to chaos. These fears, based as they are on ethnic beliefs, are terribly difficult to dispel. I stand, if I may, by my faith that world unity can be achieved only through the bringing together of the different units, merging them into a whole that will retain the individual characteristics of the parts, while it strives toward ecumenical service and progress.

I cannot find a more adequate and eloquent illustration of my belief than the artistry of the mosaics. I am sure we all recall the beauty of them as we have seen them in Constantinople, Ravenna, Venice, Athens. This splendid work of the mosaics has survived centuries and has equally impressed and inspired humble souls and great artists. Mosaics are, as we know, made of small pieces of glass or stone, all different in shape and color. There is not one exactly like the other. But through the art of lovingly and thoughtfully assembling, with steadfast purpose, these disparate units, the artist has achieved a masterpiece.

I believe that all enterprises of love can find in this a meaning and an inspiration.

It is, in my belief, through open-minded communication that we shall be able, at one and the same time, to keep individuality alive and to cultivate and strengthen human relations, by preventing isolation—another word for barrenness.

Communication is essential to freedom of thought, of inquiry, and of action. It stiffens and becomes inflexible in the dogmatic climate of autocracy. It fragments and runs to waste in an environment of anarchy. It thrives in the liberal, open-eyed, and open-minded atmosphere of democracy.

Aristotle, describing the ideal state in his *Politics*, sees it as a community one could perceive at a glance from a hilltop. Although the human community through the centuries has become infinitely more complex and interrelated, Aristotle's vision is still pertinent to our thought. For we, like Aristotle, must be aware that only when all are able to know the components of the "city" that is our worldwide community—the many diverse interests of its citizens, the points they have in common, their vital needs, their skills, their aims, their hopes and beliefs and fears—only then can people advance.

Is it not evident that we now have in communication a resource that can strengthen our understanding of the immensities—and that through it we can be made aware, as from the top of an imaginary hill, of the human pulse of the whole world at every moment? This awareness will, I firmly believe, nurture humanity's possibilities for happiness. In this way, through mutual understanding, recognition of individual duties and rights, served by communication in all its forms and aspects, we shall be able to realize the dream of one of the great presidents of the United States—the dream of "living together and working together in the same world."

8. The Wonders of Creativity

SALWA C. NASSAR

[LEBANON]

T HE CREATIVE INDIVIDUAL is an organic and dynamic part of his society. In creating ideas, discovering principles, developing techniques and methods, expressing himself in literature or the arts, or in understanding human affairs, he interacts with the social structure in which he lives. Consequently the social changes that are taking place in the world today—and which are mainly due to the achievements of the creative individual himself—are bound to have serious influence on him as an individual and on his creative activity.

In ancient times, in some parts of the world, and more recently in other areas, men of thought and makers of ideas did not interact much with all layers of their societies: They tended to stand apart from the common run of their fellow men. Financial and moral support came to them mainly from the ruling authorities—from kings, pharaohs, caliphs, emperors, and sometimes from religious institutions or from the educated elite. The motivation of the creative individual, which springs primarily from his natural curiosity, received its nourishment from such sources, while his inspiration came from the natural phenomena and from traditional and religious themes around him. The impact of his creativity was necessarily confined to a small group, and consequently both his responsibility and his influence were highly limited.

Certain communities in the Near East have always venerated scholarship and learning, either by tradition or by reason of being enjoined to do so by their religion. Their veneration led at times to great cultural productivity, as during the golden era of Islam between the ninth and the twelfth centuries A.D., when Arabic scholarship preserved much of the Greek heritage and created much that was original in science and mathematics. Yet, later on, the pious respect for learning became formal and sterile.

History is rich with evidence of increased creativity as a result of the intermingling of cultures and the fresh fusion of ideas. Language itself was the fruit of such interaction. The alphabet, that most efficient basis of communication, was the result of an interaction between Phoenician ingenuity and both the Arcadian cuneiform script (the Rasshamra alphabet) and the Egyptian hieroglyphic-determinative system (the proto-Sinaitic Byblos alphabet). The concept-symbol correspondence in Babylonian algebra resulted from the fusion of the Semitic and the Sumerian cultures. The rise of Greek mathematics and science occurred at a time of close intermingling between the Greeks and the people of the Orient. Such interactions, however, came mostly through traders and warriors and were thus necessarily limited.

At present, the awakening of the masses, the democratization of society, the advancement of technology, the increase of knowledge, and the greater complexity of economic relationships—all have resulted in an increased interdependence between the creative individual and society, as well as between society and society. At the same time these factors themselves are initiated primarily by the achievements of the artist, the scientist, and the educator. Scientific discovery, in particular, is at the root of almost every change in the world.

The interaction of societies on a world scale has been enhanced, and contacts among creative individuals throughout the world are now possible.

These worldwide contacts lead to mutual inspiration and healthy competition among men of thought, thus resulting in greater productivity and speedier establishment of facts. The results of a physics experiment, for instance, may be announced at some conference, and within weeks—or even days —data in support or denial begin to appear from laboratories in different parts of the world. Related experiments are planned and collectively performed at times, such as the International Geophysical Research which began on a very modest scale in 1957 and which continues today on a much wider scale. This project, as it developed, brought together the thinking of people from many countries and in almost every field of knowledge—fields such as astronomy, economics, electronics, space medicine, solid state physics, and the like. Investigation is thus made possible in fields where one specialization alone might not be adequate. Without this world cooperation, the results would have been far less complete, and this experiment gives us beautiful evidence of the cooperation that is possible among scientists, irrespective of the political ideologies held by their nations.

While the tremendous increase of knowledge in our time has demanded a high degree of specialization, with knowledge being broken up into a number of strictly defined compartments, nonetheless the various fields of specialization continue to depend on another. There is hardly a physical discovery that has been made in isolation. In nuclear science, for instance, new developments have depended, and still depend, on knowledge accumulated through the work of scientists in related branches. Such interdependence enhances creativity through the exchange of human experience. The relevance of various fields of knowledge to one another broadens the sympathies of the scientist and enriches the inspiration of the artist. (Too much interdependence, however, may lead in certain fields to uniformity—a danger that must be guarded against.)

All this increase of contact among different societies—and between the creative individual and society—has given this creative individual today a much greater field to act upon. Artist and scientist have come to exert a great influence on the public, an influence that increases the opportunities as well as the responsibilities and the dangers they are likely to face. The public, for instance, which at present enjoys the fruits of technological developments is disposed to support the financing of scientific research. But those who have the power to allocate funds for research may hamper the freedom of the creative individual in his search for truth. And the creative individual, in trying to influence and please his ever growing public, may yield to the demands of his society—sacrificing quality for quantity, precision for urgency, depth for superficiality, beauty for convenience.

The intellectual in a newly developing community may face still further dangers and difficulties. There is the pressure of nationalistic sensitivity with which he has to reckon, or with which he may be himself involved (although this same nationalism may inspire creativity). There is also the tendency to confuse science and technology, even among people expected to know the difference, and a society may develop which draws on the benefits of technology without undergoing the rigors of scientific research. Finally, there are language difficulties in those countries where the national language is not yet adequate for modern scientific expression. It seems to me that this last is a very serious problem—and one to which we have not given enough attention.

To counteract these dangers and to meet the needs of the ever increasing world population, knowledge must be brought to the public. Modern means of communication, themselves the results of scientific discovery and development, make this possible. Radio, television, the theater, and the modern press are powerful tools for the spread of knowledge and culture among ordinary men who had little contact with ideas before the advent of these mass media. Such media can certainly be abused, but for good or for evil they are instruments of power which intellectual leaders can use to diffuse knowledge as the basis for thought, sound judgment, and esthetic appreciation. And while such use of mass media will not create the maker of ideas, it can kindle the spark of creativity in a potential creator.

Finally, I would like to point out that all creativity involves a three-sided relationship. There is interaction between creative individual and creative individual, between creative individual and society, and between society and society. All three sides are essential for the structure, and the strength of the whole depends on the strength of each side.

And a situation of external and internal equilibrium is necessary for the continued fostering of creativity. The discoverer of a certain physical principle or phenomenon, for example, cannot be held responsible for how other creators develop his discovery, nor for whether society applies it for constructive or destructive purposes. Thus when James Clerk Maxwell put forth his theory of electromagnetic radiations, he could hardly anticipate that fifty years later, radar, a device made on the basis of his theory, would save nations from destruction and millions of lives. Nor could Madame Curie anticipate, as she spent days and nights trying to isolate a few millicuries of radium from tons of ore, that half a century later whole communities would be working in industries based on her discovery. Nor could Ernest Rutherford expect, when he first disintegrated the nucleus of the atom, that a quarter of a century later his discovery would lead to a chain reaction capable of destroying one hundred thousand people in one shot—or that his techniques eventually would be used in blood transfusions saving millions of lives.

Such are the infinite wonders of creativity, whose encouragement, in the unfolding destiny of humanity, must ever remain a supreme purpose of education.

9. The Conditions
of Creativity

PARVIN BIRJANDI

[IRAN]

MY PAPER is not strictly scientific in nature, since I could not possibly suggest that all its statements are based on pure research. Rather do I offer a few tentative observations, speculations, and suppositions on the subject of creative individual development—and the implications of these thoughts for education.

Let us first examine the key word "creativity." The well-known psychologist Klopfer describes one aspect of creativity as "the constructive use of the imaginal resources at the person's disposal, resulting ideally in a flexible and constructive manipulation of the possibilities of the reality situation in solving problems and in arriving at fuller satisfaction of needs."*

This description links creative ability closely to the environment in which it exists, and it plainly implies the important influence this environment may have in facilitating or in hampering the creative powers within the individual. It is a scientifically accepted fact that every emotionally healthy

---

* Bruno Klopfer *et al.*, *Developments in the Rorschach Technique* (Yonkers, N.Y.: World Book Company, 1954, 1956).

individual, with a normal or above normal amount of intelligence, possesses some creative ability in different degrees. This is the gift of heredity. But what happens to this ability is strictly a function of the environment. "Man," in the words of L. K. Frank, "is an organized complexity that exists in a surrounding field with which it is dynamically and reciprocally related."*

If we examine, then, some of the physical surroundings with which known creative genius has been "dynamically" and "reciprocally" related, perhaps we can understand something about the kind of environment conducive to the development of creativity.

The Golden Age of Greece is one of the outstanding periods in history that produced great creative thinkers. Historians tell us that this was a period of relative peace and great prosperity for the Greeks. Freedom of speech existed, and philosophers were admired and respected.

Looking at the old Persian Empire and studying the conditions under which Darius the Great built his monumental Persepolis, a truly great masterpiece of artistic creation, we find again that prosperity, freedom, and justice, together with well-organized financial support and encouragement on the part of the kings, were determinants in encouraging the artists to bring forth the best of their abilities.

Would it be fair, therefore, to say that peace, prosperity, justice, and freedom, within the nation or society, are enough for the emergence of creativity? It would certainly not be a far-fetched proposition. And yet—examining the other side of the picture—we notice creative artists of the highest order living in the darkest moments of the histories of their nations or under extremely unfavorable social conditions. Hafez, the unparalleled Persian poet, from whom Goethe admits gaining

---

* L. K. Frank, *Individual Development* (Garden City, N.Y.: Doubleday & Co., 1955).

inspiration, lived after the dreadful Mongolian invasion of Iran, when the country had sunk into the lowest depths of corruption and decay. He lived in utter poverty. No ruler supported his poetry for long, because Hafez could not keep up a false pretense of admiration, nor could he follow and be bound by the generally accepted religious rules and regulations of his society. He lived, like most other geniuses, beyond his times and never regarded the prevailing ideas of his fathers as indestructible or absolute.

In the poetry of Hafez we can see the penetrating search of a truly great thinker, trying to rip open the dark door of uncertainty. True, moments of despair overcome him when he feels failure to discover the truth he seeks. And a pessimism casts its shadow upon his poetry, as he talks of the expanse of the problems with which he has to cope. But he never gives way to despair, for in his own words:

> Though lost in the vast wilderness of uncertainty,
> I hear the far-away chimes of a caravan.

Eventually he does reach the conclusion that "The Chalice of Jam"—the cup that reveals the secreta of the world—has been in his own possession all the while he has been looking for it and begging it from others. He comes to perceive that the doors of Truth are opened to man only from within—through meditation.

Can we say, then, that unfavorable social conditions killed creative genius in Hafez? Nothing would be further from the truth.

To illuminate the problem, let us go to our psychological knowledge. Clinical experience, observations, and research indicate that repressed desires, if strong enough, usually come to the foreground of consciousness, appearing in some form of disguise. An examination of the history of creativity in man will reveal the same trend. When faced with oppression and social prohibitions, the lesser artists or those with weaker creative urges have perhaps dropped out and been destroyed. But where the amount and force and flow of constructive imaginal energy has been strong and uncontrollable, the artist has always devised various methods of self-expression. Satires and symbolic expressions in literature can be placed in works of this category. The exquisite and finely detailed Iranian miniatures and the elaborately designed tile work of Persian mosques seem to reflect the direct sublimation of the Iranian artist faced with religious and political prohibitions.

We can suggest, therefore, that the creative urge in man has always proved stronger than the factors that—inadvertently or intentionally—have tried to suppress or eradicate it.

At this point the question might be raised as to why some of man's most important inventions have been produced at times of war and stress, and why, even in normal competitive situations, the amount of creativity and achievement increases.

This phenomenon might be explained in the light of two independent psychological studies. McClelland has shown how importantly motivation arising from parental attitudes toward intellectual achievement affects both the school grades and the ambition of bright high-school students to go on to college.* The less keen this parental motivation, the less is the effort toward achievement. At the same time, another psychologist, Zeigarnik, in a completely different set of studies, reached the conclusion that unfinished tasks produce a tension within the individual that spurs him on toward completion of them.†

Can we not, then, by combining the findings of these two experiments, suggest that during times of stress—whether produced by war or lesser events of a competitive nature or

---

* David C. McClelland, *et al.*, *Talent and Society* (Princeton: Van Nostrand, 1958).

† Zeigarnik, "Uber das Behlten von erledigten und unerledigten Handlungen." Psych. Forsch, LX, pp. 1–85, 1927.

even activated by simple personal needs—tension is produced which drives the person toward accomplishment and the use of all resources at his disposal, thereby reducing the tension within him? In other words, tension, induced through motivation, tends to increase creativity.

At this point, however, a great danger presents itself—namely, overpressure. Frank warns that certain practices of child rearing, attempting to hurry the child forward, deny him the opportunity to live and function freely at an early stage of development.* Such efforts to bring about precocious maturation may be likened to an effort to skip or shorten some phase of the fetal development. In a similar manner, effort to expedite creativity through exerting extra pressure can produce an inverse reaction completely fatal to the creativity of the individual. For it is a well established psychological fact that anxiety above a certain level is the greatest deterrent to the free flow of creative energy.

Now, at this point, I would like to make a cultural comparison quite likely to invite controversy. As I view the problem of creativity within the two cultures with which I am most closely acquainted, the American and the Iranian, certain points stand out in both countries which, in my opinion, prove detrimental to creative development. One essential point to be remembered in this comparison is that the words "Persian" and "American" denote the masses of the people in each country and not the select few who stand apart from the general pattern of their society.

We can almost place these two countries at the opposite end of the same continuum. In America society has advanced to such a high degree of organization—has become so well defined and elaborated—that creativity suffers interference because of too much direction. Too many ready-made facilities are too easily available. Recreation for the masses is too

---

* Frank, *op. cit.*

uniform. Everyone falls so much into the pattern of a pre-planned life that little time is left for experimentation. Within the framework of freedom and the rights of the individual, so much security is offered by society that the challenge to use these freedoms in everyday life tends to be forgotten. Too many experts do the thinking for the people, and the result of that work is so accessible to the ordinary person that he does not have to exert himself toward further achievement of original ideas. In other words, if an American individual follows the accepted rules and regulations of his society, on a superficial level, his needs can be easily met. And through a lack of demand upon his creative potentials, he can become too lazy to think for himself.

In Iran, however, people are still faced with the primary needs of life. Higher processes of thinking and second-level needs are meaningless to most of them. For numerous reasons our educational system does not offer students the broad general information and background so essential to the development of creative thinking. Nor do our school children get the necessary freedom of expression and opportunity for bringing forth their own ideas. Considering the fact that only 20 per cent of our population is literate, and that our school children are the luckiest group as far as mental development goes, you can see the extent of the vacuum in which our people live, with regard to even the rudimentary essentials for development of their creative powers. Although the old order is changing now in Iran, creativity in most fields, except for the arts perhaps, finds little welcome and appreciation: it is usually met with a wall of resistance born of centuries of tradition and deep fear of the unknown.

Yet change is coming to Iran, through the impact of civilization and the use of Western products, upsetting all the old value systems so rapidly that little time is left for the people to absorb and integrate the new values into their lives. The greater part of the mental energy of our people is being used either in resistance to the oncoming changes or in rapid successive adaptations to new situations. Along with feelings of being caught unprepared and a general sense of bewilderment, fear, uncertainty, and frustration conspire to block creativity.

Evidently a middle-of-the-way solution has to be reached. But where do we leave off the resistance and chaos of old underdeveloped societies—and where do we stop, along our road of progress, to provide the best conditions for development of creativity?

The answer, in my opinion, should be sought in a scientific approach to the problem through research.

As we look toward the new world's community and the generations who are to lead it and to live in it, the role and the encouragement of creativity clearly emerge as supremely challenging educational jobs. The vast advances made in the medical field may prove of use in helping to raise the level of creativity through prenatal care and development. The role of hormones, vitamins, and minerals in the mental development of the fetus have been shown in various studies. But, once born, the child becomes the creature of an environment that must bring forth and train the best within him.

This environment at first consists of the parents who lay the foundations of mental health for their child. Mental health, in my opinion as a psychologist, and mental health alone, provides people with the moral courage, honesty, and determination to seek the truth—and the will and conviction for its expression. Such mental balance enables a thinker to use to capacity whatever creative power lies within him. Thus, I think that the greatest responsibility for creativity in the future falls on the parents of tomorrow—to raise their children in homes that will provide them with the necessary ingredients of sound mental health.

As the child grows up and goes to school, entering a larger environment, the factors that are important in bringing creative ability to the foreground seem to be as follows:

First: providing the means for a broad general education

and informational background. We know of no creative thinker with a limited outlook. There are often by-products of certain creative endeavors more important than the product itself. Training children to keep an open outlook, and providing opportunities for them to experiment in various fields when they are young, open up new vistas and give them the broad educational background essential to creativity.

Second: providing a motivation. The child needs goals—some clear notion of where he is going and what his life is going to mean. These goals are at first personal, but as time goes on, social perspectives develop. At all stages of growth, the providing of motives and the setting of directions are necessary to give the child security and objectives in life. This does not mean, of course, that we should limit the child's freedom of experimentation or impose activities on him. But in my experience with primary school art students, when total freedom of choice was allowed, children usually resorted to easy and trite subjects such as a flower or a car. But given some direction (such as, "What you saw at the movies"), they would surprise with the amount of creativity and innermost feelings reflected in their work.

Third: providing means of specialization. Creation does not just happen. No creation, on the higher level, is possible without laborious training and a strict command of the field. It is necessary therefore to provide the means of specialization—experts, equipment, funds, and, above all, teachers.

Certain considerations should be kept in mind if teachers are to be successful in training children to think creatively. Merely repetitive insistence on injecting thoughts and habits can block children from creativity. Too much direction, logic, over meticulousness, pedantry, and superficial attention to unnecessary detail can stifle the play of intuition. At the same time observation must be encouraged, as the key that unlocks the doors of creation. Teaching children to observe and to draw conclusions is basic to further use of creative abilities.

There is, of course, no substitute for work—and its trials. Children learn through work, and whoever works is bound to make mistakes. These mistakes are valuable. Teach children to benefit by former errors and use their experiences in overcoming problems. To make children feel guilty over errors is one sure way to stop their creative urge.

A period of free and spontaneous diversion is necessary. It has been observed in highly talented people that after hard work there often occur periods of revolt, sheer idleness, and renunciation of customary ways of life. Therefore, any expectation that children maintain an ever productive stream would be folly.

Little time is given to children these days to stay alone with their own thoughts. Too many planned, prefabricated diversions can paralyze their minds. Provide the child with the challenge of entertaining himself during free, unrushed time. A harried routine is neither intellectually stimulating nor creatively productive.

We should remember, above all, that the creative child is as much a healthy, normal usual child as anyone else. He need not be a "namby-pamby" or an unrigorous recluse overly mothered because of his supposedly extreme sensitivity.

In conclusion: If I were to choose one word to be used as the keynote to an educational system ideally encouraging of creative ability I would suggest: *balance.*

This means: balance between freedom and direction, progress and stability, work and play. And it means: seeking perfection without pedantry, being constructively motivated without overanxiety, sensing tension for production without feeling harried—and balance between a down-to-earth sense of reality and those visions of new vistas that can come only to a creative mind.

PART III

Conference Addresses

10. The Breakthrough to Modernity

BARBARA WARD

[GREAT BRITAIN]

WE ALL CAN quickly agree, I imagine, on one fact: The crisis of our times affects all of us, whatever our culture, whatever our background, whatever our nationality, whatever our race. We are all involved now in the drama of humanity—and involved in a way that is totally inescapable. Our lives are knit together, and whatever our background, we share a common humanity which is more threatened than it has ever been in the history of man.

I do not see that we can have any other background to our deliberations than this profound sense of our belonging together, of our working and suffering together, of our ultimate interdependence. This common destiny is not just a matter of the hydrogen bomb and of all the risks and hazards of nuclear conflict. True, it is here that our interdependence reaches its most extreme point. But I believe we all are bound together in another deeper and more far-reaching sense. Today all the races of mankind and all the human societies on the face of the globe are involved in the same kind of profound historical transformation. The only analogy that comes to my mind is that millenniums ago the beginnings of settled agriculture forced the old hunting, fishing, and food-gathering societies back to the fringes of the settled world. Then gradually began the adventure of civilization which was based, in its deepest physical roots, upon the settled methods of agriculture. In the last two or three hundred years we have become involved in a new movement of seismic change in the topography of the human race. All of us—whether we are of West or East, whether we are Communist or non-Communist—are moving forward to the modern society based on science and technology. And this change is an even greater—and far more sudden—break with the past than the shift from nomadic life to the settled life of agriculture millenniums ago.

Some nations are, as it were, through the sound barrier of modernization; other nations are coming up to the point of breakthrough. But all of us, without exception, are involved in this new kind of society, and we are all experimenting with vast problems of modernization based upon the application of man's reason and man's scientific method to practically everything he does. The change covers every aspect of his life. Nothing is left out. Not an institution, not an idea escapes re-examination. All are being turned upside down, rethought, reapplied, found wanting, discarded. There is not an area of life in which the forces of change are not fiercely, drivingly, unpredictably at work.

The fundamental technological change, the change that affects all our methods of production, is that of applying massive capital—or savings—to the techniques evolved by science, and thereby enormously increasing the productivity of man's work and his capacity to produce wealth. This process goes far beyond what is usually called the industrial revolution. We pick on industry because it is what seems to be most obviously new. But the application of reason and science to human procedures affects every sphere of the economy. In fact, nowhere is it more penetrating, and nowhere does it have a more profound effect, than in agriculture.

You can indeed argue that the transformation of farming, even more than the new structures of industry, underlines the technological and scientific character of our new society. It is not only the techniques that have to be changed. Aims, too, must be revolutionized. The old aim of agriculture lay in subsistence and status. The new agriculture is increasingly aimed at the production of food for the market and the maximum return on farming capital. But to change from subsistence to the market is an intensely difficult revolution, for it demands sharp changes both in attitude and in organization. Naturally, if you have been farming for two thousand years in the ways of your fathers, you do not take kindly to the idea of changing over in a few decades to quite new methods. This, incidentally, is why the building up of industry can be less of a problem than the transformation of agriculture. In industry you begin from scratch. The switch from the artisan in his village workshop to developed factory industry entails the physical movement of people from the countryside to the big cities. The move in itself breaks the cake of custom and begins to create workers who can adapt to change. Agriculture you have to change *in situ*—among the old ways, the old neighbors, the old landmarks.

The new techniques are not confined to changed methods of production, however, and another whole field of change has opened up in education. The new technological society will not work—unless it is an educated society. For the first time we see states in which everyone is literate, in which everyone has access to ideas, to reading matter. (They also have access, of course, to reading matter that gives them no ideas—but nonetheless the access is there.) At the same time a broadening of technical skills is changing the whole character of education. We see it in the West, we see it in Russia:

the gradual increase in the scope and esteem of the scientific and technological disciplines, and, if not a decay in the humanities, at least the coming of the day when the humanities have only a complementary place beside a vastly expanded scientific field.

If we turn to politics, once again the change is complete. Old hereditary patterns of leadership were more or less adequate to the unchanging reality of subsistence agriculture. Old men are natural leaders in a society where fidelity to tradition is the highest wisdom. In a world of change, on the contrary, men are needed who can cope with the new kind of society. A modernizing elite has to emerge to exercise genuine gifts of leadership absolutely indispensable to lead the people from the known to the unknown, from static society to dynamic society.

All over the world today men are having to exercise this type of leadership: to take their peoples on from settled habits which go back thousands of years, and to plunge them into the opportunities and risks of the modernizing revolution. The people they lead are usually bewildered by the upheavals through which they have to pass—one reason why, I believe, the twentieth century has seen so many myth makers among its leaders. When the people do not understand the chaos of change about them, they need passionately to be given a pattern or a myth to bring apparent order into the confusion. If all the old landmarks are disappearing, you grasp at the great simplifications to explain to you what is happening: the victory of the proletariat, the end of imperialism, the *Führer-prinzip*, blood and soil. And this need for myths, coupled with widening literacy, has made the twentieth century a century of propaganda on a scale never seen before.

But perhaps the greatest change is psychological and lies in the way men and women look at the purpose of their lives. The drives behind a society that is maximizing wealth are quite different from the attitudes of a settled society content with subsistence, and now all round the world they are sparking what Adlai Stevenson has called "the revolution of rising expectations." Because of it millions upon millions of human beings now believe that tomorrow can and, indeed, should be better than today—whereas the greatest reach of the old wisdom was to believe that if tomorrow was no worse, you were very fortunate.

We all, then, the whole human race, are caught up in this great process of change and modernization. We all march in the same column. We may be placed at different points along the route. But we cannot escape our common destination.

How did we come to begin this journey? If we can look back to the beginnings of the road, it may give us some idea of where we are and where we are going—and what are the contrasts between various methods of achieving the modernization that all now desire. For there is a significant division, at present, between a modernization that follows a pragmatic and flexible, even open pattern and another kind of modernization represented in this century largely by communism, with its techniques of forced, accelerated, and directed economic and social change. The contrast between these varying methods of introducing modern ways may throw a significant light on contemporary problems of modernization and suggest the circumstances in which the milder or the tougher methods of change are more likely to be effective.

Let us begin with the change of leadership, for it is crucial. Until society is dominated by people who are going to make scientific changes, to compel industrial development, and to undertake the saving and investing both imply, such changes will simply not take place. In the West, where modernization was first launched, the adjustment of leadership goes back a long way: The idea of constitutional government, the rule of law, and a certain underlying thrust of equality began, early in the Middle Ages, to create a political breakthrough of what we now call the middle class. The plurality of power, arising from the fact that emperor and pope competed for loyalty at the top of the system, also encouraged decentralized power to develop at other levels. The establishment of organized city communes and corporations goes back to the thirteenth century, and the first consultation between the sovereign and the citizens he was about to tax goes back to the fourteenth century. Thus, at an early stage there were signs that the middle class would have an effective field of economic and social operation outside the interventions of arbitrary power from above. I recall some phrases in the diaries of an official of the East India Company who went out to India when, in the eighteenth century, the power of the Moghul emperors had begun to decline. This is how he describes the attitude of the monarch toward his people. His habit is to "look on the growing riches of a subject as boys look on a bird's nest. He eyes their progress with impatience, then comes with a spoiler's hand and ravishes the fruits of their labour." Clearly, with such a political background, merchants are not likely to accumulate capital, and they are not likely to enjoy that self-confidence of leadership necessary to produce a large element of directed change in society. Thus, the emergence of a merchant class with enough elbow room, with security to expand trade and reinvest the proceeds, is one of the early factors in the modernization of the West.

One should also add at this point the cultural changes that occurred at the time of the Reformation. The Puritan revolution stressed the belief that man's handiwork also shows forth the work of God, and that, as a consequence, to work hard, to earn a great deal of money, is a way of pursuing the glory of God as well as the success of your enterprise. And the belief was accompanied by a feeling, also nurtured in Puritanism, that money once earned should not be spent on worldly enjoyments. An enormous drive for accumulation was paradoxically combined with an equally powerful inhibition on spending. It is hard to imagine a better recipe for capital accumulation.

The limits to its productive use, however, were set by the smallness of the number of techniques in which one could invest in those days. No one invests simply for the sake of postponing consumption. At the end of investment must lie the hope of greater productivity, but better productivity implies better techniques. If the outer limits of your technology are the skill of a hand, the speed of a horse, the energy of wind and water, or the heat of charcoal, then clearly the range of techniques in which to invest savings is severely limited.

Up to the eighteenth century this absence of advanced technology continued to limit the amount of capital that could be usefully invested, but there then occurred another decisive mutation in human thought. In western Europe, largely as a result of the Wars of Religion, men abandoned theological speculation for a passionate concern with the natural sciences. Such a shift was possible in the West because, in some measure, Christianity has been a "this-world" religion—having deep within it the Jewish idea that the world is God's handiwork, as well as the Greek version of the whole universe operating according to orderly law. But undoubtedly the great impetus to scientific thinking was, to a real degree, a revulsion against dogmatic ways of thought which divided people desperately, quickened by a feeling that in the safe, solid experimentation of natural science, men of good will could reunite. An immediate consequence of the new fervor for research was to lay bare a vast new range of technologies. And all over England, in the eighteenth century, country gentlemen, dukes, parsons, artisans, bankers, often sitting in a little laboratory in their back garden, were at work trying out new ways of doing things.

With this opening up of new techniques, with savings expanding and becoming more institutionalized, with country banking beginning to spread all over England, the essential components of the new society—new leaders, capital, technology—created a breakthrough to the modern society. The whole process occurred pragmatically, experimentally. If you had asked any of these men what they were doing, they would probably have told you they were making money. What, in fact, they were doing was founding the new order of the modern world in which the maximization of wealth, the creation of new methods of production, the search for productivity and for new methods of expanding the stream of income became, for the first time in human history, the dominant interests in human society.

This first breakthrough was not, however, the last. The ideas and attitudes that had made possible the assumption of leadership by the middle classes continued their ferment, and after the 1880's in Britain—and in other modernizing communities—it was the turn of the workers to attain relative power, relative influence, and a greater measure of well-being. This transition has proved fully as decisive as the earlier one. It was not, after all, at all clear at the time that the change could be made peacefully—within the framework of constitutional politics and pragmatic economics. In the first half of the nineteenth century our Western society had been going through what Marx calls "the phase of primitive accumulation," and this had proved a very rugged experience.

It is worth our while to look at this phase a little more carefully, for it is the one through which most of the developing world is passing or is about to pass today. The starting point is the fact that the preindustrial society is, by definition, poor, simply because the number of ways in which wealth can be produced are still restricted. However wealthy the citizens of the rising middle class may be in a personal sense, they simply do not command sufficient capital to do more than just begin. The reason for this simply lies in the enormous scale of capital needed to complete the transformation of the economy. If agriculture is to be transformed, for example, better crops must be introduced—better seeds, better fertilizers, more farm machinery, better draining and aligning of the fields. Then, if the new agricultural and industrial products are to reach the market, there has to be a radical transformation of the entire transport system. In England the Duke of Bridgewater's inspired canal building, the creation of turnpike roads, the opening up of new ports, and later on, the crucial development of railways—all played an essential part in getting the system into momentum. And all were, in terms of capital, enormously expensive. These capital overheads or "infrastructure" of transport and energy can account for as much as 60 per cent of the necessary spending in the early days of growth.

There is, too, another form of essential overhead—the capital invested in men, women, and children. At first the economy could get on with rough, untrained labor. But the moment any degree of sophistication enters into agricultural and industrial processes, society has to begin to educate on a massive scale. And the more sophisticated our system has become, of course, the more we need to educate people to grasp and work it. From its roots in general literacy, on to the present need for a steadily higher percentage of trained graduates, modern education has demanded large expenditures—and no developing economy can afford to devote less than, say, 4 per cent of its total national income to the advancement of education.

Only when capital is available for modern farming, for infrastructure, and for a massive expansion in education is it really worth while to envisage the further expenditures needed for industry. All this adds up to an immense demand for capital. Moreover, in the early stages of growth much of this capital is needed simultaneously. Unless there is general momentum in investment, the economy does not achieve a steady movement toward general modernization. Instead, you see the pattern that is so evident all around the colonial world: with a small segment modernized here and another modernized there (a port, an export industry, a few planta- tions), the beginnings of modern education—but none of the modernization on a sufficient scale for each investment to begin sustaining all the others in a sort of upward spiral of expansion.

In short, unless a society can contrive a fairly massive input of capital at the beginning of modernization, it is likely to miss the momentum of genuine growth. Professor Walt Rostow has given us a vivid analogy of the process in his concept of "take-off." He compares a developing economy with an aircraft. Unless the plane reaches a certain speed on the runway, it does not take off: If you live in Boston, you simply run into Boston Bay. So it is with the economy.

The scale of capital needed in the early stages of growth explains the political stresses through which emergent so- cieties have to pass. Society has to be compelled to save when it is still in a preindustrial, and therefore prewealthy, condition. The early stages of industrializations have been on the whole nasty, brutish, and, if a nation is lucky, short, but more often, long. The workers who crowded into the new industrial cities of England or France or Germany, and the migrants who poured across the Atlantic to America, con- tributed enormously to the capital growth of the community. But for decades they received very little in return in terms of rising consumption. This was for a simple reason. Since their competition and general defenselessness held wages down, the whole surplus created by the fabulous productivity of the new machines, in terms of profit, went back to the entre- preneurs who would reinvest it.

We can see with hindsight that their reinvestment was the means whereby capital on a sufficient scale for the original take-off was achieved. The channeling of the entire surplus to the reinvestors meant that the capital base of the whole economy could expand. If consumption had risen, capital formation would have been retarded. The breakthrough might even not have occurred. But to the workers struggling on subsistence wages, the whole process looked like nothing but exploitation. And it was at that time that Marx first formulated his theory of the capitalist system.

After this first phase of brutal saving, the whole industrial machine was in being. After 1860 in Britain there was a measure of "trickle-down," as we may call it now. Productivity was such that profits and wages could both go up. Trade union organizers saw to it that wages did. The enlarged popular vote ended the helplessness of the poor.

Yet a dilemma remained—a dilemma we still have not entirely resolved. Since a wage is also a cost, there has long been a tendency for rising wages to push costs up to the point at which the profits to be earned by the enterprise no longer seem worth the risk. High wages are needed to create the mass demand that alone will clear the market of the goods the machines can pour out. But high wages may also reduce profit margins to a point where the entrepreneur will not invest. Between the two world wars a period of stagnation, for these reasons, overtook the West.

Today we have found some way out of this dilemma—pragmatically, as usual. Part of the answer lies in the extension of Social Security that insures that mass purchasing power is not curtailed, even in times of recession. But the major change is the more or less general decision that the maintenance of employment, and therefore of investment, cannot be left solely to the play of the profit motive. If private initiative is not employing the community's resources to the full, the government, by fiscal or monetary or any other suitable policies, must do so instead. The war undoubtedly hastened the learning of these lessons, since the stimulus war production gave to expansion revealed what a slack there had been before, and the over-full employment of the war economy created new levels in purchasing power to give the postwar economy a species of jet-assisted start. Since 1949, too, all Western economies have carried the extra spur of an arms program. But whatever the reasons for the new approach, the West—pragmatically and without planning to do so—has evolved a new kind of economy: a mixed economy in which government and private enterprise on the whole cooperate and in which the full use of resources is a legitimate concern of government.

And still another series of pragmatic policies insured that the new economy would also operate at the international level. The remarkable achievement of the Marshall Plan was to transfer this new kind of mixed economy to western Europe which, between the wars, had been the most stagnant and depressed area in the capitalist system. There the rise of a new industrial phoenix from the ashes of an earlier industrialism is one of the great success stories of our time.

Thus, in short, as we consider the development of our economy, we should think not of a single breakthrough to modernization but of a series of critical thresholds which have to be passed or crucial rungs on the ladder which have to be climbed. Now, even as we have moved on to another phase, we need not doubt that further steps, too, lie ahead. We never know from one day to the next what new breakthroughs science may be preparing for us. Our system is still ill equipped to deal with absolute abundance. Can a price system be maintained while we smother in surpluses? We need foresee no shortage of dilemmas in the years ahead.

Nonetheless, in its long-drawn-out, pragmatic fashion, the West has produced a society that, if not wholly just, at least is tolerably just; which, if not wholly equal in opportunity, is more equal than anything produced so far; and which quite clearly, in its experimental shape, is a going concern, not at a loss to achieve broad institutional change.

And now we must look at another way of carrying through

the processes of modernization. The classic example of planned, directed, forced-draft development is, of course, Russia.

Here the more pragmatic and experimental methods were not able to accomplish the change, and the first reason may well have been decisive: There was no easy breakthrough to new leadership. As late as 1917 Russia remained autocratic and bureaucratic in its political structure, with a rather small Russian middle class of no experience comparable to the long evolution in the Western world. It was not until the middle of the nineteenth century that even the serfs were emancipated in Russia. Neither on the land nor in the cities, then, were there sufficient "new men" to provide spontaneous modern leadership on a sufficient scale or of a decisive kind.

This, in turn, helped to explain the fact that a large part of Russia's economic development was stimulated by foreign enterprise and financed by foreign capital. In a sense, you could say that before 1914 Russia had some of the marks of a semicolonial appendage of western Europe. It showed the same face of partial, patchy modernization—a factory here, an export crop there, some infrastructure, some modern education—which we find all around the developing world today. And it showed, too, some of the same political tensions. There was a mood, indeed, of more than discontent: there was a sense of society running into an impasse. The reaction in Russia contained within it the shape of things to come: nihilism and revolutionary radicalism among the narrow but growing middle class, above all among the students who represented the growing point of modernization in Russian society.

On top of all this turmoil and intellectual confusion came the First World War—to break up traditional Russia in awful agonies of destruction and carnage. The Bolshevik coup succeeded because, in a situation of total confusion, here were men determined to take over power and believing, with the blind belief of absolute faith, that they knew what to do with power when they had achieved it. This seems to be a law of history. In situations of confusion, anarchy, and social collapse, the man—or the small group of men—with a clear idea of what he is doing and with a sense that he can interpret the times, has an overwhelming chance of seizing power, even when he is a megalomaniac like Hitler. Now Lenin was a man of high intelligence and of enormous will power. And the brilliance with which he and his group exploited the last closing, collapsing phases of the European war is a superb lesson in the tactics and strategy of political manipulation.

But the lesson covers a paradox. Lenin, in fact, did not know what to do next, for although he had manipulated a revolution successfully, it was not the revolution he had been taught to expect. Marx had prophesied that communism would come in a fully developed industrial country. Since the capitalists would have done all the work of building a modernized structure, it would remain only for the workers to seize it, run it, and distribute the output properly. It would be as simple as that. But, of course, in Russia after 1917 even the beginnings of modernization had been run down to ruin by the war. For the first decade after the seizure of power I think we can say that the Communist Revolution in Russia fumbled about, trying to find out what it was to do. Here was a vast peasant country with little infrastructure, insufficient education, and only the beginnings of industry. And Lenin died, the problem unsolved.

It was Lenin's successor, Stalin, who came up with the answer and devised what we now see to be an alternative method of modernization. I sometimes wonder whether the model for it was not the massive, centralized mobilization of men and capital for the production of munitions in the West between 1916 and 1918. Whatever the pattern, Stalin mobilized the Russian nation and compelled it, in the first five-year plans, to go through the phase of primitive accumulation.

The plans aimed at forced-draft modernization—in transport, in industry, in education. And the essence of the plan was to insure that the capital saved by the Russian people was adequate to the scale of economic expansion envisaged. Estimates for the scale of capital accumulation in England during the critical phase of primitive accumulation are all guesswork, but a rough estimate has been made that between perhaps 15 and 18 per cent of the national income was finally saved. If a man's personal income is below one hundred dollars a year, such a saving is a grinding business. But in Russia we reckon that annual saving went up to 25 or 30 per cent of national income. The pains and sufferings were appalling, particularly in the countryside. But the saving did produce, in ten short years, sufficient capital equipment and a sufficient industrial structure to withstand the onslaught of Hitler in 1941. Other breakthroughs may have been more resourceful —as was the Japanese. Others, notably the American, may have been as quick. But few faced Russia's desperate need to recover from one war only to fight another. The urgency gave a special edge to the chosen methods of total planning, total regulation, total regimentation, and total savings— methods more rigorous than any that went before.

Today, with the terrors and horrors and wastage of the last war left behind, we do not know, in the current atmosphere of cold war, what use Russia will make of its breakthrough to modernity. Will the aim be power and world conquest? Or is there any hope of the next phase following the Western pattern and looking toward the mass-consumption economy? Such a change involves many social and political modifications—more representation for the working class who make up the mass of consumers, far more awareness of their interest, far more readiness to spend on welfare, particularly for the aged and for the unorganized workers. These changes have occurred in the West. Are there any signs that Khrushchev is trying to achieve the Russian version of a broadening of the base of the economy? It is true that after Khrushchev came to power, he introduced some minimum wage regulation, put more emphasis on old age pensions, and has talked of more consumer goods. These may be the first harbingers of a time when the needs of the consumer will rate rather more highly in the Russian plans. We may also hope and pray that the Russians may ultimately be lured into a disarmament agreement by the need to release far more of Russia's now established industrial output to the consumer. And yet, despite all this, we must equally recognize that Soviet emphasis on power and world dominion still seem to presuppose an economy primarily devoted to the piling up of national strength.

Let us now take these two methods—the pragmatic, improvised methods of the West and the forced-draft drive of the Russians—and note some of the points they have in common. They are both methods of modernization. Both involve a decisive change in leadership, with power going to new groups. Whether you call them commissars and delegates, or whether you call them managers and elected representatives, they represent a clear break from the traditional idea of kingly rulers, flanked by the warriors, the priests, and the aristocratic landed interests—the form of rule typical of human society during most of its history. Both societies evolved a technique (which now lies behind them) of securing that indispensable early massive capital accumulation. Both societies set immense store by literacy and scientific education, often ruthlessly and extravagantly applying more and more scientific techniques to the production of their goods. And in both societies I would take a most significant trait to be this steady rise in the range of research and in the application of rational and scientific methods to wider and wider areas of human experience.

What they do *not* have in common can, I think, be most quickly seen by discerning which societies are more likely to use the one or the other method of modernization. Looser, more pragmatic methods of modernization imply—in the first place—at least the promise of an active, educated, and self-confident middle, or managerial and professional, class. Thus the reason why the prospects for change by evolutionary methods seem good in, say, India and Pakistan lies in the fact that the Indian subcontinent has already had over a hundred years' experience of modern education. Now I do not mean to suggest that before this process of modernization began, India had no great tradition of learning. On the contrary, one could argue that its peoples were more cultured than the masses in the West today. There is a gap we all have to recognize between true culture and a somewhat bastard literacy. But what I am talking about here is the type of education and experience needed in building up the modern technological and scientific state. There is no doubt that pragmatic methods stand a clearer chance of achieving modernization in nations where modern education has some depth and duration, and where the professions are expanding and an adequate administrative cadre can take on the responsibilities of decentralized power. It is the old story of leadership.

This leads up to the next condition for this kind of growth: that the country be genuinely interested in some strategy of development. In any state in which traditional leadership with its paramount interest in status, conspicuous consumption, or public grandeur is still in control, the chances of modernization by moderate means are virtually nil. In such societies farming tends to be feudal and static. Business enterprise concentrates on real estate and monopoly gains. Tax policies "soak the poor." Expenditure on education is marginal. Such societies do not evolve. They simply wait for a violent revolution. Where, on the contrary, the government is bent on change, where it encourages land reform and fosters agricultural production for the market, where it builds up a solid infrastructure in power and transport, supports a steadily widening area of industrial growth, gives a really big push to literacy, and adopts policies of taxation and fiscal reform to foster all these aims—there the chances of growth by evolution are really promising. Once again, the Indian subcontinent offers an example of modernizing governments bent on change by evolution.

Nonetheless, all such societies face a fearsome challenge in the early stages of the attempt. How can they achieve primitive capital accumulation without demanding so great a sacrifice from the people that their attachment to open institutions falls away? Indeed, can the sacrifice be asked for realistically in terms of free choice? A man on an income of sixty dollars a year will not readily vote himself out of 15 per cent of it. And if production rises by so much, he will not save it. He will eat it.

This is the basic reason why the period of primitive capital accumulation has almost nowhere been accomplished within the framework of popular consent. Certainly nobody asked the workers in early industrial Britain whether they wanted to save. I doubt if anyone asked the migrants in nineteenth-century America whether they were in favor of the system that transferred so much of the fruits of their labors to other hands. But today in many developing countries the audacious experiment of combining primitive accumulation with a free vote is being attempted. In India government rests wholly upon public consent, and this, for me, is an essential part of the drama of development in the subcontinent.

This brings us to a new point. Even those countries that have adopted a genuine strategy of development may, so long as they attempt an open society based on free choice, face a crucial and decisive obstacle. Without sufficient savings, they will not achieve momentum; without momentum, they may modernize here and modernize there, but they will not reach the point of take-off into the modern technological society. It is at this stage that external economic assistance can become crucial. Aid in the form of capital from abroad serves two essential purposes: It provides essential foreign exchange, and it lessens the need for draconian saving inside the developing economy. Provided the capital is brought in to supplement a genuine local effort toward development, it can be a key element in insuring that the country passes through the phase of primitive accumulation without too much curtailment of liberal aims and institutions. A number of economies are in this phase—among them those of India, Pakistan, Mexico, Brazil, Argentina, possibly Egypt. But such programs of foreign aid should not be simply a haphazard dumping of capital on countries that cannot absorb it—as some programs have proved to be. On the contrary, they can be an essential supplement—hastening change and preserving an open, uncoercive pattern of politics.

But Western programs of assistance can do more than act as economic agents and catalysts. They have a profoundly significant part to play in changing the political climate of world opinion. Most of the developing countries today lie in ex-colonial areas. Understandably enough, one of their main political preoccupations is a profound uneasiness lest the imperialism that went out by the political front door may now be creeping stealthily in again at the back door of economic aid. Needless to say, the Communists encourage this fear.

A great deal therefore depends upon the context in which programs of economic assistance are worked out. They have to be seen as part of mankind's general effort to achieve the modern economy—not as a campaign to make clients or stop Communists. Within such a framework economic aid can be human and tolerable. It has a certain dignity and conveys a certain vision for the future. It is not condescension. It expresses a Western understanding that the drama of development in the emergent world is a familiar drama in which the

West has already played a part and can now take on a new and more generous role. So conceived, economic assistance becomes the negation—if you will excuse the Marxist jargon —of imperialism itself. And it can cushion developing societies against the need to indulge in heroic, totalitarian domestic saving.

If, now, we ask ourselves where, on the contrary, the forced-draft methods of communism are most likely to be adopted in the search for modernization, the simplest answer is to pick out those communities whose conditions most resemble the state of Russia in 1917. Let me quickly recall conditions there. A thrust of investment from western Europe had helped to create the first stirrings of modernization— some export crops, a transport system, growing cities, some industry. But the mass of the people lived in a stagnant, depressed, feudal countryside. Modern education was extensive enough to create a discouraged elite, but not large enough to underpin a rising middle class. On top of all this, war crushed whatever momentum had been achieved, and in the resulting chaos a determined group of Communists seized a revolution that was sparked not by Marxism but by a savage desire for peace and for land reform. These conditions were repeated almost precisely in China with, in 1949, the same result. And I think where similar conditions are repeated, the temptation to follow a Communist solution will be strong. Even where the revolution itself is not Marxist in inspiration, its leaders may well adopt communism simply because the pattern is in being. And this can be the case in Cuba. Thus, on all the uncertain fringes of the modernizing world, the struggle between the various forms of the open society and the stricter Communist pattern will continue, with Communist methods enjoying some strong advantages simply because they offer a pattern for chaos.

This is not to say that communism will always be an organizer of chaos. The Chinese experiment is still insecure.

The Communist record in agriculture is abysmal. The histories of the minor communisms of the world are still to be worked out, and eastern Europe does not so far suggest irresistible success. Moreover, I, for one, do not believe in a monolithic communism. I think there will be many different kinds of communism—as different, say, as the Yugoslav type or the Polish type. The varieties will be more luxuriant as different nations develop according to their own profound cultural inheritance.

For the time being, however, the contest between the rival methods of modernization is bound to continue in all those areas where order is precarious, where changes in political structure and in social organization are difficult to achieve. We cannot avoid the contest. It is built into our present modernizing phase of world history. This, I take it, is the competition Mr. Khrushchev refers to in his idea of "peaceful coexistence." And it will cease only when the revolution of modernization is more or less complete—or when, tragically, the competition has led to the final disaster of atomic war.

This risk is the most pregnant fact we have to consider. No doubt it would be fascinating at this point to look at some of the problems that lie beyond modernization. All that our science and technology do is, after all, to build a new machine for living. This is not a negligible achievement. It creates the possibility of lifting the age-old burdens of mankind—hunger, poverty, ignorance, ill health. Yet it is already clear that neither Communist society nor the open society have so far produced any answers to some of the most urgent challenges in our world. Each of us can make a personal list. For me, it begins with the appalling, heart-destroying ugliness of so much of our urban life. Moscow is as ugly as Manchester—there is nothing to choose between them. Yet we add to America every year a city the size of Philadelphia. Urbanization is carried forward so formlessly and shapelessly, with so much attention to real estate values and so little to decent human living, that the end result is an inhuman sub-urban sprawl. Yet we know that the population of the world is going up by billions in the next forty to fifty years. Most of those billions are going to live in cities, and most of the cities will look like the appalling cities we live in now. The imagination boggles at the thought of most of mankind con-demned to a life so lacking in the larger esthetic satisfactions of civilization. None of our methods of modernization so far has been able to resist the sucking pull of existing facilities, and the big city becomes a cancerous symbol of uncon-trollable growth.

But more important than such problems of the future is the problem of whether we have any future at all. The competition and rivalry of systems which we know as the Cold War contain perpetually within them the possibility of hot war. Compared with this, every other issue is strictly secondary. Here must be the final focus of our interest.

Where can we look in our search for the framework of survival? So far, in only one area have we been able, in our political life, to reconcile divergent interests and to see the peace secured. This area is, of course, domestic society. We have no other analogy. We know no other way by which men can live together and not kill each other. But over large areas this minimum of security has been achieved. The American federation covers an entire continent. And historically one quarter of the human race has continued to live over long periods within an orderly civil society. I refer to the imperial system of China which did give peaceful rule to more people over longer periods than any other human order. An encour-aging fact is that the imperial framework was maintained without any great intervention in local affairs.

But it did provide for three fundamental preconditions of an orderly political society. First of all, it allowed for the peaceful settlement of disputes by law, custom, arbitration, and conciliation—the whole process backed and supported by a police force. Second, public works and famine relief were a preliminary sketch of the idea of the general welfare, the sense within the community of some sharing of burdens and advantages. Third, the community was held together by a certain underlying trust: There was normally enough confidence and good will between citizens to enable them to take the roughness off the inevitable acerbities of social life and maintain a sense of community.

I would suggest, therefore, that our chief task today is to transfer to the world at large the three fundamentals of domestic peace. When we talk of general and complete disarmament, we deal in a generalized way with the first condition—the peaceful settlement of disputes. Heaven knows the prospects look bleak enough. Yet I have no doubt that when the English King Henry II began the attempt to limit feudal violence and stop the barons from cutting each other up, the establishment of the King's Peace must have looked remote indeed.

And perhaps this limited idea of the King's Peace is a fruitful one. Henry established certain routes and certain areas under the protection of royal officers. Offenses there came under the court's jurisdiction. They were policed and controlled. General justice would come later. A concrete start was made. Today it is not difficult to pick out the areas of major disturbance where the collapse of old empires and the thrust of new ones most threaten the peace. Indochina, parts of the Middle East, the heart of Africa, central Europe —these are more perilous than the lawless roads of medieval England. Possibly here, under United Nations auspices, we could seek—as a preliminary to general disarmament—to establish "stand-off" areas, in which, by agreement, the arbitrament of issues will not be by force.

When we consider such possibilities, I do not think it is enough to say the Communists will never agree. I think we also have to ask ourselves to what extent any sovereign state is likely to agree. Behind our talk of general disarmament (which we all accept in some measure as a necessity of the future) there are some tough decisions to be taken in terms of abridging sovereignty. We cannot preserve unbridled power for our states while theoretically accepting the need for international juridical solutions and a strengthening of the arm of the United Nations to act as police force in international disputes. I sometimes wonder whether we fully face these implications ourselves and the need to abrogate sovereignty—not simply because of the destructiveness of warfare, but also because every move toward more modern forms of investment and production increases the worldwide interdependence of our economic systems. We have become a physical community of getting and spending. But we lack the civic and moral institutions to leaven our material unification. We have a body; we lack a soul.

This brings us to the issue of the general welfare. Can we undertake our economic assistance programs on a sufficiently large and long-term basis to see in them the expression of our solidarity with the rest of the human race? The Western world now carries the inescapable responsibilities of great wealth. Evasion of them must lead to the moral decay that has overtaken groups and people in the past when they proposed that those who had no bread should eat cake. But in this instance the acceptance of a moral responsibility also carries with it great practical and political possibilities. Given effective economic aid, the turbulent time of early modernization could be shortened, and nation after nation launched on the great upward swing of sustained growth. If we pursued this end with the kind of energy that we have put in the past into the waging of war, has it struck you that in the course of the next twenty years a great majority of the developing countries of the world would be drawn across the threshold of modernization and achieve the framework of a functioning economy? And if the process were accomplished with pragmatic and open methods, the next phase of man's history would begin, not under the star of dogmatism and despotism, but with open prospects for the spirit of man.

Last of all, let us consider the factor of trust. Certainly we cannot create it quickly. We are more divided perhaps than were Catholic and Protestant in Europe in the sixteenth century, and we do not yet see what mutation of ideas can help us to transcend the ugly gulf between us which envenoms every problem.

But at least can we, who claim a pragmatic approach to politics, base our discourse on something more solid than our ideological fears? Can we try to remember that there can be a demonology of anticommunism as well as a demonology of communism? It is true that the Communists insist on projecting onto the world the dark shadows of events that are long since gone. They accuse us of being capitalists of the stamp of the 1840's, and they accuse us of being imperialists in the image of the 1890's. And apparently these masks of terror which they have made for themselves hide from them the fact that Western society is now based on a mixed welfare economy, and that the wealthy West, far from being imperialist in the old sense, may not export enough capital abroad to do the essential job of development.

The masks are there: This we cannot deny. But can we at least, on our side, seek to lay off our own masks and talk more directly to the condition of man? Can we overcome the natural arrogance of being sure we are right, and remember instead that all of us—Communist and non-Communist, black or white or yellow, Eastern and Western—belong to a threatened humanity and have to see, behind all the masks, the face of a brother who is in as great a danger as we ourselves?

Here, I think, we have to call on our deepest traditions. Our societies in the past have, none of them, been societies in which the great ethical ideals of man have been absent. It is the tragedy of our modernization that, in our hurry and intoxicating material success, we have been blinded—by the practical achievements of technology and the immediate vistas of wealth—into forgetting the purpose of all this development: the good society in which men will have the elbow room to pursue the nobler purposes of life.

The definitions of nobility vary in our cultures. But none of them denies, I think, the primacy of disinterested love. And it is the special challenge of our times that we learn to think of men as brothers—in a world where modernization is drawing us all together, a world that forbids us to evolve policies, or think of our future, in isolation from the human race. The new unit in which we have to operate—morally, socially, and economically—is the great family of man. If this concept means more to us than Fourth of July oratory, more than mere lip service, if it deeply inspires our policies and our initiatives, may we not be able to reach across the gulf that divides the world, may we not be able to discover, even behind the masks that communism and anticommunism throw up, the solidarity that we share as members of the human family?

I do not know whether we can succeed.

But I am convinced that there is nothing more worth trying for in this troubled world.

11. The Power
of Education

ALVA MYRDAL

[SWEDEN]

I WISH IMMEDIATELY to focus our attention on a central proposition, instead of letting it be reached gradually as a conclusion. It is this:

The paramount role for achieving any kind of development —and most definitely any development great enough to be judged beneficial to our whole world of the future—belongs to education.

All progress achieved by mankind so far has been decisively dependent on this one lever—the improving of the quality of the human resources. This truth can most simply and clearly be seen in the fact that countries so vastly different in their levels of living are *not* that different in *natural* resources.

The term "education" is, of course, to be understood in its widest sense: as any systematic influencing of people's knowledge, skills, and attitudes. Such education not only serves obvious utilitarian purposes; it also—perhaps most imperatively—cultivates and strengthens the will and the capacity of all peoples to accept worldwide responsibilities and to escape self-destruction in this world of multiplying material benefits and menaces, the increasing technological com-

137

plexity that our modern magic has created. Such education, at the same time, is not only a means but an end in itself. The question can never be one only of education of manpower—but of man himself. "For what is a man profited, if he shall gain the whole world, and lose his own soul?" We must do both: gain the whole world and still retain that capacity for creativity, that sublime sensibility to the new, which is vital to the human being.

Let us briefly look at some historical illustrations as supporting evidence of our central thesis. For history is quite adamant in its verdict on the role of education.

It is true, of course, that my country, Sweden, is often praised for its high standard of living, and I have come to believe that the secret behind our success can be reduced to one fact: We were fortunate enough to get universal literacy —through compulsory schooling covering the total population—half a century before we were seriously drawn into the orbit of industrialization. But lest I be suspected of being chauvinistic—and also to isolate the factor of education much more succinctly—I would rather use Denmark as a test case. For this is a country that has had so many fewer natural resources than Sweden—and, as a matter of fact, many fewer than most of the now so-called "underdeveloped" parts of the world. Even Denmark's only asset—its soil—can certainly not measure up to the fertility of large parts of Africa and Asia.

Here, then, is a country that, until the middle of the last century, was just a traditional one, mainly living on its own agricultural production for subsistence while also selling some exportable surplus on the world market. It had emerged from feudal conditions only rather recently: The bondage of the peasants, which forbade all males over the age of four to move from their place of birth, had been abolished by law only in 1788. When that country was suddenly, in the middle of the last century, faced with ruin through undercutting competition from the increased production in Russia and, more particularly, in the United States and the new overseas territories, Denmark did not accept defeat but met the challenge by carrying through a masterly reorganization of its farm economy. The corn which had become cheap was turned into fodder, and a new, highly competitive farm economy was built up as an internationally specialized one, on the basis of animal foodstuffs, through dairy farming and processing of the new agricultural products. All this involved not only a change of production techniques, requiring more individualized efforts by each farmer, but also a new organization for quick and dependable marketing. This was realized in the form of cooperatives—cooperative dairies, cooperative slaughterhouses, cooperative export agencies—for which there existed at that time few, if any, prototypes in the whole world.

Since that time Danish agriculture has continued to be perfected as a modern rationalized industry, importing its raw materials (fodder and fertilizers) and exporting its finished agrarian products, which make up more than half of the country's foreign earnings—although only a quarter of the working population of this small country needs to be engaged in the rural sector.

But this is not all: The momentum has been kept up and spread to other fields. Today Denmark has also become prominent as an industrial nation, with its exports of industrial goods (cement, machinery, ships) earning millions of dollars, and its engineering firms being in demand for construction jobs the world over.

From the point of view of the Danes themselves, the satisfaction derived from these historic efforts in economic growth has translated itself into a high level of living. Among the ranking countries in per capita national income, Denmark (according to United Nations figures for 1952 to 1954) was topped only by the United States, Canada, Switzerland, Sweden, and Australia. If weight were given not only to average income but also to the equality of its distribution and to other elements of a welfare state, such as social security, Denmark would rank even higher.

There can be no doubt that the carrying through of this remarkable "industrial revolution" in Danish agriculture, particularly by the development of cooperative methods, was rendered possible only because the Danish population was already rather thoroughly prepared by education. No other country had so early and so comprehensively instituted compulsory schooling. Already in the last decades of the eighteenth century, simultaneously with the emancipation from feudalism, and even more in the first decades of the nineteenth century, when the country was still certainly poor and underdeveloped by our present standards, liberal ideas about the value of education began to fire the imagination of Danish leaders. A royal decree of 1814 made schooling compulsory for all children, sanctioned the establishment of state schools in all localities, and even stipulated a fine for parents who did not keep their children in school. Thus, when the great decisions had to be taken and implemented to change the nation's economy, the challenge could be met by a people who already had behind it a generation of practically universal literacy. And, alongside the public education system, there was further created, beginning in the 1840's, a widespread system of voluntary adult education through residential colleges for rural youth, supplemented by similar but more vocational agrarian schools.

The facts of Danish history, then, seem clear: Nothing, other than this grass-roots type of education could have liberated and fortified the people's economic stamina, their rational insight, and their will to cooperate.

The United States and Great Britain offer similarly striking examples of the singular role of education as a prerequisite for national development. There is no doubt that the tremendous pace of American economic growth can be related to the extraordinary interest already taken in education as early as the colonial period. The case of Great Britain is a little different. Although Great Britain started far earlier than any other society on the path of rapid economic development, there came a time, toward the middle of the last century, when her rate of progress was being overtaken by countries like Germany, at times also by France, and by the United States. One crucial reason for this, a reason of strategic importance, was that England, during this period, lagged behind in primary education for all the people (despite its centers of higher learning for a select few), while countries like the United States and Germany, Holland and Scandinavia, put very great stress on getting their educational systems broadly based. At the same time the interest in practical, manual, and technical training also had an earlier breakthrough in the United States, Germany, and Scandinavia than in most other countries, certainly including Great Britain.

Leave the Western world entirely, and look at Asia. No more plain proof of the role of education exists than Japan. The difference between that country and any of its Asian neighbors is most definitely visible in its purposeful cultivation of skills. And, of course, it tops all other Asian countries with its literacy figures above 90 per cent.

Finally, and most contemporarily, there is this dramatic indication of the validity of my thesis: the present "educational race" between the Soviet Union and the United States. The two giant powers of the world have undoubtedly realized that their ultimate strength will depend mainly on their new conquests in science and on their people, their skills, their ingenuity. Just as the United States in the last century was making possible such enormous forward strides by educating and training its population, so we are seeing the same process at work in this century in the Soviet Union—achieving what must be called, if we recall the status of the pre-revolution Russian people, another miracle of development, chiefly by raising the educational standards and certainly not by an import of capital. When a rigidly planned economy devotes such relatively great sums to education, does this not flash a signal that education is investment and not consumption?

I have culled all these examples of the value of education to social and economic growth from the economically advanced countries rather than from the underdeveloped ones. I have done so deliberately. For one thing, the process of growth of these advanced countries has reached well-nigh a summit, and one is therefore much more on the safe side in trying to analyze the factors responsible for such success. Moreover, it seems wise to single out, for special attention by the underdeveloped countries, who look for guide lines from the history of others, the important truth that there is *one* factor of growth fairly independent of natural resources and therefore most easily and inexpensively introduced. And that factor is education.

When education is thus seen as being of such primary importance to a people's development, the fact becomes even more acutely evident that the present-day world is sharply divided between haves and have-nots. The gap is great—and widening. Some countries, largely in the Occident, are well endowed not only with all kinds of material riches but also with fairly abundant resources for education. Other countries, belonging to the underdeveloped regions in the Orient and in the Southern Hemisphere, are not only hungry, diseased, poverty-ridden; they are also sorely lacking in the very educational facilities so necessary to start to put matters right.

The supporting material for these statements is harsh and abundant. I need merely allude to the fact that while countries such as Denmark have a rate of 100 per cent literacy, the comparable figure for Nepal is hardly more than 5 per cent; and even in so comparatively advanced a country as India, it is just climbing from 20 to 25 per cent. As for annual per capita income, despite all the flaws in its calculations, it can serve to show a dramatic difference when, in a country like India, it hovers about sixty dollars, while in so many Western countries it is at least twenty-five times higher: some fifteen hundred dollars in Sweden, some two thousand dollars in the United States.

How is our world going to be able to sustain such contrast —and such tension? To my mind—and there are many who are beginning to think likewise—this division, between a privileged half and an underprivileged half of mankind, is looming as a much more formidable risk for our future destiny than the tension of present-day economic ideologies or political blocs. From this realization stems the now rather feverish preoccupation with plans to help develop the under-developed regions. But when we search for the *means,* we come right up against a dilemma: Granted that education will promote economic development, education also pre-supposes the prior availability of certain economic resources. How is this vicious circle to be broken?

At this point, I must in all honesty pause and confess that there is not complete agreement on the thesis that raising the educational level is a prerequisite for attaining economic de-velopment. There are, in fact, two kinds of criticism often voiced.

The first line of criticism comes from the economists who hold that investment in human resources is too slow in maturing and that it cannot, therefore, be given primary attention. Only after a generation or two, it is argued, will a general provision of primary education result in a fairly large cadre of persons with higher technical or otherwise specialized education. Economic development should, there-fore, first rely on certain shortcuts for accumulating capital aimed at raising the national income almost immediately;

and thereafter increased resources can and should be gradually more and more devoted to raising educational levels.

Any such discussion of priorities can sound like another variation on the chicken-and-the-egg theme. But I venture to dissent from these economists who would seem to strive to bypass—to race around—the factor of education. Where are the other magic shortcuts, unless a country has easily extracted and highly priced raw materials to export? In general, agriculture has to be reformed to render higher yields, and industrialization has to be initiated. But education is needed for both. As for the time factor: The building of a fairly efficient educational edifice does not require an extraordinarily long period in comparison with the building of dams and railroads, or steel mills and oil exploration, or irrigation and electrification schemes—for all of which some ten or even twenty years must often be envisaged.

The second line of criticism against an apparently too optimistic emphasis on education brings us into deeper water. It comes from the philosophers, historians, and anthropologists who question the acceptability of the very value scale that makes "development" equivalent with "progress" and assumes that such development really is the generally accepted "goal" of all peoples. In short, we come up against the notorious dichotomy between values sometimes called Eastern and Western, or—somewhat better—Occidental and Oriental, or sometimes just described as "material" and "spiritual."

I suggest that we must approach this problem not as a matter of any arbitrary a priori choice but as a question of values that must be submitted to the underdeveloped countries themselves. Who are the "we" to choose for the "them"?

It is true, of course, that in many parts of the underdeveloped countries, particularly among their rural masses, there is no real and ready acceptance of our chain of values—development, growth, raising levels of living—all implying perpetual change. And there lies a deep difficulty hidden here. For change can hardly be truly evaluated where change is unknown. Of course, most people want to improve their economic conditions somewhat; but they may only want, perhaps, more of the same thing that they have always known. Thus, a people's demands may be reduced to small improvements and accretions which do not revolutionize production. Whether this is due to a lack of imagination or is a conscious predilection, the fact remains that large masses in the world do not look forward with eagerness to a setting of goals that become constantly higher and higher. In short, the "economic man," of whom both capitalism and Marxism have been so enamored, is certainly not a popular figure in the underdeveloped world.

What should be done practically, as we face attitudes so different from ours—far less acquisitive and competitive, valuing conformity to old patterns so much more and change so much less? If the answer be the one sometimes proffered by anthropologist-romanticists—that is, to try to stave off change as being only "disruptive"—then the solution would be to establish these underdeveloped societies as some kind of cultural reservation. But is that what we want? Is it what *they* want?

In this dilemma there is no easy solution. I can only suggest that the choice must be made by the people themselves. To make it, they need a clear appreciation of the costs imposed by the different alternatives. This implies the only attitude worthy of Homo sapiens—namely, an *inquisitive* one. Such an attitude stands equally far from the romantic view—the respecting of traditional values so much that even dirt and disease are kept in place—as from the missionary concept of zealously introducing all and sundry goods, services, techniques, and ideas which we have happened to esteem as good in our kind of society.

In short, instead of prescribing one course or another, we

can do only two things. We can foster a truly inquisitive attitude toward the realities of the choices before a new nation. And we can promote—as the one great antidote to any unduly harsh or overpowering cultural pressures—the education that gives to the people the power and capacity to make their own choices.

If we accept these two pragmatic purposes, we have, of course, actually accepted one supreme value—namely, rationality. And here I am taking the stand, shared by an increasing number of people, that the supposed cleavage between totally different Eastern and Western value spheres is a false conception. And this I want to defend to the bitter end—as I have been endeavoring to do in all my actual contacts between the living East and the living West—my conviction that *rationality*, the supreme value of *Vernunft*, can never be claimed by any part of the globe as a kind of private and parochial inheritance. On the contrary: It is truly universal. It belongs to mankind—as truly in Africa and the Americas as in Europe, as much in India as in Italy, as surely in China as in Greece. Any *special* values to be ascribed to one of these various cultural spheres must be more narrowly defined and circumscribed than this supreme value.

The role of education, then, becomes manifold. It enables peoples of the newly developing countries to choose their own direction, instead of having it chosen for them by dominant influences from the sphere of Western modernization. At the same time education is also needed in order to safeguard appreciation of certain traditional values. And there is a wide margin for such values, so that no one way of doing things can claim to be evidently more rational than any other—whether you excel in curry dishes or French cuisine, wear saris or Chanel suits, play the piano or the sarod, create Gothic vaults or Moslem mosaics. Education helps the candid choosing of values in this sphere by fostering self-assurance, and we must never deprive the newly born and developing nations of pride in their own.

Rationality certainly will not stifle this pride. It simply allows the choice between various means of satisfying social needs, while it gives ample room to faithfulness toward the traditions that can survive this test.

I have laid such stress on this matter of choice because of the fact that *planning* is accepted as a necessary form, indeed a duty, for all countries now entering the phase of modernization. For the course of development in these countries need not be a repetition of what has earlier happened in countries already advanced—whether the latter's policies be called capitalistic or Marxist—but rather a creation of new social forms.

For the newer countries this means that it should be possible to weigh in a rational fashion their resources, their values, and thus combine their goals and means in a much more efficient way than we ever were able to do. It further means that it should be possible for them to take effective steps to rectify such developmental trends as may be judged to be creating unbalance in the growth process. Thus the new countries might, in fact, have a so much more painless course of development—all other things being equal.

But all such planning—again—presupposes education. While in many Western countries, to some extent, education was allowed to lag, the introduction of education in the early stages of development is a *must* for the planned societies. In these societies, communication must be established so that the planning endeavors reach out to, and call forth a response from, the whole population. If a nation is not made one social body through education, there undoubtedly exists a risk that the people will be shepherded like an unthinking herd through all the new processes, led by decrees of more or less unintentional dictators. The point so often raised in warnings about planned societies—that planning might lead to slavery —is valid only if popular ignorance is allowed to prevail or regimentation is enforced by dictatorship. Citizens made conscious and active by education need not run the risk of losing their freedom.

But the educational factor is urgent. For the newly developing countries have made a much more hazardous approach to democracy than the countries of the West in a comparable stage—by their attempt to introduce democracy at the very start of their modern growth. Democracy as a goal is one thing, but its immediate implementation through universal suffrage in an illiterate society is quite another. The risks of bossism, of undue influences, of manipulated scares, and of fantastic promises are only too real. The one way to counteract them is by education.

Both planning and education must join to meet another challenge confronting the countries developing in our scientific era—the sharply accelerated population growth. Any progress achieved in these countries by great efforts at modernization—by investments in industry and intensification of agriculture—is, to a horrifying extent, "consumed" by the ever increasing numbers in the population. The fact that the modern scientific approach through medical advances becomes automatically geared to death control but not to birth control is responsible for this unhappy unbalance. This can be remedied only by an enlightenment enabling the citizens to plan their families. Only an intelligent, alert, educated population can take this responsibility for its own destiny.

I have, to this point, tried to stress that any major effort to speed a nation's development and, at the same time, to anchor it to democratic values should be centered in the field of education.

Where do we go from here? We need to single out the basic elements in the development process which education can promote more concertedly.

I believe these elements—these dimensions of change—can roughly be summarized in three words: mobility, enterprise, rationality. Should we not always measure what education is achieving with these criteria as yardsticks? First, the factor of *mobility:* Education can, as can nothing else, prepare individuals in an old social order for physical, social, and mental mobility, or, rather, "fungibility"—that is, the readiness to accept change and to act with purpose in new circumstances. Second, the factor of *enterprise:* Again, education uniquely can stir people to take initiative for new action, to introduce a daily ounce of improvement in their immediate environment, to release that measure of new energy necessary to speed a society's development. And the factor of *rationality:* What but education can inspire the habit to probe instead of believe, to analyze critically instead of blindly accept, to weigh alternatives and choose with eyes open toward the future?

Let us now examine, briefly but explicitly, how well these criteria of progress actually *are* being met. And let us first look at the pattern of action *within* the underdeveloped countries themselves.

The primary question must necessarily be whether the development plans of various national governments, in these countries, take sufficiently radical and efficient steps to speed processes of change through education. I am afraid that a summary judgment must be that as yet they do not.

Of the three factors of change just mentioned, perhaps the one most widely promoted in socio-economic plans is the first one, mobility—largely because it promotes itself. In fact, so clearly and closely is the development process connected with introduction of the means for mobility that, I sincerely believe, a basic measure of ongoing change can be a kind of "index of wheels." For example, just as the introduction of horse-drawn vehicles was once an enormous step forward for our Egyptian and Greek ancestors, so a similar onset of change can be observed today all over the Indian subcontinent—with the coming of the bicycle. Production and sale of bicycles mark the one economic sector where actual realization has far overreached the targets set in the five-year plans.

But all modern mobility, challenging the individual with constantly new experience—new modes of living, new ways of speaking, new beliefs—has rarely been adequately prepared by education. Education would, I believe, spell the essential difference between simple physical mobility—sheer movements of people—and fungibility. To give a telling example: it has been found in India that the jobs as drivers of long-distance lorries are offered as particularly suitable for "graduates"—that is, the few who have had some schooling. The simple reason for this is that they are the ones who can read the signs, check the papers, and psychologically cope with unfamiliar environments. Should this not be read as a simple lesson that vastly more education is needed everywhere to smooth the path of mobility?

Even less seems to have been done to foster systematically, through education, the element of enterprise. The lack of entrepreneurship, and the inertia of the masses are objects for complaints all over the world, clearly contributing to the slowness of development. But which government can be found that has used its educational system as a great lever for getting the people action-minded? Few sights fill one with so much melancholy as seeing the all too few schools in an underdeveloped region being plagued by our cast-off methods of mentally passive pedagogics—while all the hammering, building, and experimentation are going on in the schools of the West, whose people are already so stirred by the lust for activity!

As for the third constituent of change, the element of rationality, this is least of all consciously fostered. If people are to be moved along a path to modernization, considerably more of a scientific—that is, a nonsuperstitious—education will have to be introduced. This must start at the village level, with corresponding reforms at all levels of education—on up to true universities not bogged down by traditionalism but opening the minds of the young to experimentation, surpassing themselves in new research, and participating in a living relationship with their societies.

What is needed, then, is a massive enterprise in which a host of related facilities are enlisted. This means concerted action for establishment of schools, for training of teachers—and better teachers—for devoting proportionately more of the educational endeavors to science and technology and medicine—with comparatively less emphasis on law and nonspecific arts and letters courses. It means, too, creating employment for the graduates, training them for more practical tasks, instituting literacy drives, planning a network of radio sets throughout the country, printing mass editions of cultural material for different levels of learning, encouraging all creative processes through debates, theatres, arts.

To date, however, one can only conclude that on the whole, due to some mysterious overemphasis on the material advance of the West, the new nations have been blinded to the tremendous need and opportunity to build new resources in their people by means that can be summarized as "cultural." The fact is that knowledge cannot be set aside for an elite. The heritage of the colonial situation, when cultural development had an enclave character, leaving the masses to subsist according to traditional ways of life, must energetically be overcome. And countries as yet not far developed will continue to suffer from a feeling that history is about to bypass them—unless new, concerted efforts are made to set them on the path of self-generating development.

All this is far more than a "school" problem, for the first level on which the path of development must be cleared is that of private life and family relations. It would be interesting to know and to measure those things in the immediate home environment, in different cultural regions, that are actually blocking progress. Meanwhile, two incipient changes in the institutional structure are aiding growth and could aid it considerably more. One is the gradual emancipation of women, the accepting of women as more equal partners and taking advantage of their advice in a freer give-and-take within family councils. The second is the effort to make simultaneous attacks on the ignorance of both children and parents. In the past, I believe, UNESCO and other educational programs have tended to overlook the necessity of introducing literacy campaigns simultaneously with primary schooling, of making this two-pronged approach concertedly in district after district. And it is almost impossible to measure the slowing of developmental impetus that can result from the gap in understanding between the youth exposed to new trends and the parent generation still steeped in and obsessed by its traditions. In short, development begins at home, quite as much as charity.

Much the same kind of self-propelled reforms can be organized also at society's next level—the village or local community. Here development can at least be initiated in learning to utilize locally available resources and, above all, local energy. The "new action" element can be simply community endeavor to clear approach roads or irrigation ditches. Perhaps the most important single effort that could be carried out without great cost is that of planting trees, at least a "village forest" for local fuel needs. (Norway is planting four hundred million trees a year. Where, in all the countries so anxious for growth, is this matched?)

As for the element of rationality, there exists at this level a unique and much needed opportunity to fortify democracy. For the primary instrument of all real democracy must be the local council, the town meeting. To thrash out neighborhood difficulties and to plan for local action is to work toward rationality and progress. And there also must quickly arise the most obvious opportunities to encourage mobility—through joint action to build roads, to install a village radio, or, above all, to start a village school. In all such ways can the local society move to meet and become part of a larger society.

Let me give a warning against possible misinterpretation here. These immediate, inexpensive improvements should never be regarded as substitutes for the larger financial aid and investment that are so sorely needed. The point is to be aware that education pays this kind of self-multiplying dividends. And—no matter how great the financial aid—any honest evaluation of development programs regularly brings out one disconcerting fact. It is the fact that instances abound when investments made, even by the best of plans, have not yielded the expected results. The explanation, I am convinced, is the failure to lay the ground floor of education.

We have—to this point—viewed the problem from the perspective of the underdeveloped countries themselves. Now we must face the question of the responsibility of the international community.

There can no longer exist any division of interest between one group of countries, the haves, and another, the havenots. We are embraced in one and the same grip of destiny. There is but one road to salvation: solidarity. This means a much greater intensity in the many endeavors aimed at redirecting the capital flow to those regions that most need investment—not only for immediately profitable enterprises, but also for investment in the infrastructures of their societies.

Against the background of the recognized need for international action, so widely discussed and increasingly implemented through a score of international agencies, let me place the main emphasis on one practical proposal. It is that the rich countries should, as a first duty, shoulder the responsibility for helping to finance education in the newly developing nations. We could well afford to pay for every single item that these nations might need from abroad: educational materials, books, libraries, equipment for training and research institutions, specialized teachers and professors. It would be highly interesting to see a comprehensive calculation of such an international budget for a great effort in education in this generation. It may well be that we would be so surprised at how little the foreign exchange component would in reality cost us that we would be willing also to contribute to the investment for local costs of education. Even to pay for a million local teachers—a true international brigade—would not be extravagant in relation to our own budgets, or when compared with what is invested in one steel mill—not to use the notorious comparison with armament costs.

There is a second duty that it is about time for us all to face as an international community of the twentieth century, and this is the duty to try to foster rationality and to suppress irrationality. Again, this duty falls specifically on the already advanced countries. As we ourselves have profited so greatly by the advance in rationality, it is painful to note how reluctant we are to wage a real fight against the obscurantism rampant all over the world. Just to cite one example: In the name of some misunderstood sense of diplomatic delicacy, nobody starts a campaign against silly astrology.

In this connection my conscience does not allow me to suppress a chain of thoughts that has become more forceful as I have seen more of different ethnic or national groups—although to mention it may seem harsh toward many cherished values of particular cultural traditions and definite dogmas of different religions. Every one of the world's institutionalized religions could give us so much more if only they removed some of their irrational, eccentric superstructures of concepts and precepts. Far too much superstition has crept into their creeds as preached by latter-day priests. Now this is no call for any anti-crusade. It would, of course, be not only blasphemous but also unrealistic to raise demands in the name of socio-economic development that any beliefs, however obscurantist, be abandoned. We do not need to make any such attacks from the outside. If only the path is followed of devoting a considerably larger share of the international development effort to education, in all its aspects, then reforms in this domain will follow by natural, inner force. A critical alertness on the part of greater and greater numbers of people will lead to the traditions becoming divested of their most particularistic notions. Thus, for example, we in the Christian churches, at least the Protestant ones, have in less than a century practically abolished the belief in the Devil and the fear of eternal condemnation to Hell. And the true leaders of religious groups everywhere will see it as their sacred duty to defend the essentials of their faiths, but—let us hope—not the nonessentials which have most often only happened to be added as a cover of dust over the original gospels.

Is it naïve to believe that now a greater world harmony is conceivable—a trend toward establishing more of a general acceptance of a "religious minimum," with regard to dogmas and ethics that determine the individual's outlook on life—leaving, of course, the ceremonial and other traditional elements intact, to preserve the diversification of cultures in the world? Anyway, for the sake of argument here, it is enough to note that some of the nonessential superstitions—which once became incorporated into religious teachings, although they were really determined by specific social needs of an earlier society, but which now constitute a hindrance not only to development but also to international understanding —are gradually becoming neutralized. This blissful process could take place more rapidly if enough effort were made toward spreading education.

It is for each confessional group to divest itself of its

ethnocentricity—of its monopolistic attitude—and to take steps in the direction of tolerating divergencies and inviting ecumenical cooperation. But particularly for the Western countries this constitutes a reminder: As, in our culture, religion has started to find an equilibrium in its coexistence with science, we should no longer allow two different approaches to the underdeveloped countries to counteract one another, even partially—that is, by exporting scientific knowledge on the one hand and Christian dogmas on the other. As science is the essence of the future wherever "development" has been chosen as the path, it must be allowed to enlighten the world, gradually overcoming superstitions and false beliefs that hinder material progress as well as understanding across cultural boundaries. Missionaries all over the world can just now be seen to be learning this. They are more and more turning their zeal away from evangelizing, more and more devoting their services to valuable technical assistance, particularly in the fields of health and education.

There is another area that cries for change: the nationalistic orientation of history and geography, amounting to an artificial restriction of our field of vision and even to a falsification of historical facts, which goes on in all our schools. With the spread of knowledge and education all over the globe, we will come to understand that no national or group interests—not even our own—can be pursued in isolation. We are coming around to the definite insight that we all share the risks and potentialities of one and the same future. Thus, it is to be hoped that the subject matter in all our schools will definitely become more internationalized—more world geography, more world history, and more sympathetic understanding of the forces molding the different nations. Here UNESCO and the international teachers' associations have already started upon an important program to guide all our schools, but without yet receiving the appropriate enthusiasm from national policy makers.

Not only the content but also the very process of education everywhere must become much more "internationalized." At the highest level this could be achieved through actual studies abroad for the elites of various countries who need specialized knowledge. There is no reason why different institutions of learning, in different parts of the world, should not take on the responsibility for becoming world centers for given scientific specializations, and open their doors to all countries. And we shall probably also have to take a new and vigorous approach to the question of languages. If we could oblige all young people in all countries to learn some language besides their own, it would be a fine guarantee that a system of international communication will be perfected and put to rational, democratic use.

In short, we must realize that there is great risk that we are not yet adapting our national institutions and our mental outlook as rapidly as necessary in the light of the technological changes that automatically push in the direction of universalization. Knowledge must become more mobile and universal. Truth must be freed from its local confines.

All this entails and demands great change not only in the external conduct of the already developed countries—but also *within* them. We face a gigantic problem in translating the idea of international solidarity into practical action in these richer countries. Our national interests are vested in fixed patterns of institutions and trade relations. What is the force in appeals for international solidarity when the terms of trade have been allowed to change, as they have been doing the last decade, in favor of the richer nations and to the disadvantage of those poorer and underdeveloped countries living by export of raw materials?

There is no doubt that such global considerations can best be made parts of firmly fixed domestic policy by the force of binding international agreements. Beyond this, I have but one suggestion—the opening, within each country, of vigilant discussion of these world issues. Thus may we learn to account publicly for the real effects of our actions not only on the national interest but also on the rest of the world, and be compelled to weigh openly and publicly whether each action of ours (such as tariff policy) helps or hinders the development we profess and pretend to desire for the underdeveloped nations.

Against this background of national problems and attitudes, there seems to be little that the smaller local community, or any citizens' group, can do. This is a great pity. For the moment, I can think of no more specific tasks for them than constantly checking the implementation of the internationalization of education in the local schools, intensifying the discussion about our international responsibilities, helping to maintain a rational attitude toward change in the world. Possibly some more concrete tasks can be found in relation to foreign students and other visitors from abroad, even a "new deal" in receiving tourists—to see that all comers partake of this most valuable community life. The loneliness of foreign students, their lack of emotional integration in the environment they visit, is something for local groups to remedy. And we should remember that these students pursuing specialized education abroad constitute the elite on whom will depend the future of their countries.

Finally, there is for us, in these most advanced countries, the challenge to do something for ourselves—to better our own lives—and so be worthier neighbors in this new world community. How do we enhance our own lives? We hardly need merely to work more. But we could probably add to the satisfaction derived from both our private and national lives if we devoted much more of our energies to re-creating constantly that extra something that gives a higher *quality* to all we have and to all we do.

I do not know if I should join in the popular chorus and pretend that the West should learn that from the East, but let me make a simplified antithesis. As *they* could produce *more* each day, *we* could produce something *better* each day. What we need for our further development is not more artifacts, more material goods. What we seem to need is a much more explicit goal for the future, to endow life with richer experiences, to deal with constantly better qualities—be they in food or furniture, art or literature, friendship or community service.

It is in these new directions—of truly serving our fellow men, enjoying our leisure in a culturally richer way, deepening our sensitivity and heightening our creativity—that we find our values moving. And it is in these directions that we can push on to even more glorious conquests.

So—remembering the adventure ahead of us, for our whole world, but remembering also the tensions that threaten to tear it asunder—I think we can do no better than to recall the prayer of the old Quaker who stood up in meeting and spoke thus: "Oh, God, reform the whole world, but please start with poor me."

12. The Survival
of Humanity

LAKSHMI N. MENON

[INDIA]

POLITICAL RELATIONSHIPS today cannot be based on a common ideology or uniformity of institutions. The old idea that adherence to certain codes of conduct or traditional principles must determine the status of a nation is a notion utterly dead. We have only to study the history, forms of government, and principles of administration of the ninety-nine members of the United Nations to realize this. This parliament of man, as Toynbee refers to it, is nothing more than the embodiment of the principle of coexistence (which is praised by those who believe in democracy as well as by those who do not believe in it). The pattern of political relationships, then, is no longer the result simply of historical ties, ethnic bonds, or common goals—but very largely of the inexorable consequences of the fear of humanity's total annihilation.

A country's relationship with other countries in the past used to be determined by its needs, traditions, prejudices, and the values it upheld and the norms it wished to maintain. The fear of atomic warfare has already annihilated the barriers raised by these traditions. As Dr. Johnson remarked: "The knowledge that you are going to be hung the next day

160

must have a marvellous effect in clearing the mind." Thus peace today is not an issue: It is neither a policy nor a program. It is the goal, but, like happiness, it is a goal that cannot be made the object of direct research. The real issue is the means to peace. For this we need not only disarmament but a new pattern of human intercourse, marked by decency and solidarity. One of the designs for such a pattern is peaceful coexistence.

Time was when a particular form of government was regarded as the ideal one, and in European history instances are not lacking of wars waged to defend monarchy and suppress the urge of peoples to participate in the governments of their countries. Among the most well-known instances are the wars of the French revolutionary period—when the monarchs of Europe combined against the French and Napoleon and, after Waterloo, resisted, sometimes successfully, sometimes unsuccessfully, every attempt everywhere in Europe to abolish monarchy. The last of such attempts was the interventionist war in Russia after the Bolshevik Revolution. Today the irresistible urges of the populaces of the world not only have been accepted with grace but have been recognized as inevitable signs of progress.

Our century has also seen, however, a new form of government, based on Marxism, emerging from the ashes of the First World War and surviving the Second World War with greater confidence and developing newer sources of strength. The government thus created and the social pattern developed by the leaders of the revolution have given a new connotation to such familiar words as "democracy" and "coexistence." Dictatorial regimes, where regimentation is legalized even in times of peace, are called "people's democracies." And "coexistence"—the supreme imperative allowing the survival of distinct cultures and societies—is given, in Communist speech, a divisive accent and meaning.

The Communist view of coexistence, since the time of

Lenin, has stemmed from a philosophy that saw conflict as the dynamic source of all development. To the Communists, coexistence means the type of cold war strategy that enables international communism to achieve its prescribed goals without shedding blood; it does not mean the existence of diverse forms of government without conflict and cooperating for common goals. Thus, in an article in *Foreign Affairs* Khrushchev emphasizes three things.* (1) We are compelled to coexist; therefore, let us live together. The alternative is destruction, which nobody desires. (2) Peaceful coexistence should develop into peaceful competition for the purpose of satisfying man's needs in the best possible way. (3) The main thing is to keep to the positions of ideological struggle without resorting to arms in order to prove that one is right. This last bit is the disturbing thing—especially when read in the context of Lenin's confident prophecy that communism would make headway "not by the force of arms but by the force of example." If there is any doubt about the Soviet interpretation of peaceful coexistence, it should be dispelled by a recent article in *Pravda* by B. Ponomaryou. Defending the Soviet policy of peaceful coexistence, he explains how Lenin regarded the policy of coexistence as the general line of foreign policy of the socialist state. After discussing the policy as helpful in national liberation movements, Ponomaryou asserts that the policy of coexistence provides opportunities for a strengthening of the socialist camp and the Communist movement—and the simultaneous weakening of the capitalist system.

All this is different from our concept of coexistence: the dream of a family of nations living together in happy comradeship. To us, coexistence means cooperation: not hostility between states of different social and economic systems, but an ideal of unity, such as we find expressed in the philosophy

---

* Nikita Khrushchev, "Peaceful Co-existence," *Foreign Affairs,* October 1959.

of a Kant and in the teaching of all the great religions of the world. Prime Minister Nehru gave eloquent expression to this concept recently, at the Fifteenth Session of the United Nations General Assembly, when he spoke of cooperation of nations:

That cooperation does not and must not mean any domination of one country by another, any coercion or compulsion forcing any country to line up with another country. Each country has something to give, and something to take from others. The moment coercion is exercised that country's freedom is not only impaired but also its growth suffers. We have to acknowledge that there is a great diversity in the world; and this variety is good and is to be encouraged, so that each country may grow and its creative impulse might have full play in accordance with its own genius.

This understanding of ours sharply contrasts with the Soviet concept of coexistence. Words do mean different things to different people! And yet the fact remains that our greatest task is to enable these contrasting definitions to—coexist.

Without practicing the Communist kind of political evangelism, we ourselves do hold to certain basic political standards. While we admit that each country must express its genius for political organization according to its ethos, civilized society has seemed to lay down certain norms, such as:

1. Freedom and peace are indispensable for harmonious development.

2. Respect for individual freedom and human rights should be guaranteed for the common man.

3. People must be given the training for the management of their affairs.

4. Representative government is accepted as the most feasible form of government which facilitates all these.

Representative government, based on adult suffrage with periodic elections and with freedom of speech and association, is still regarded as the best way of expressing the will and wishes of people. And nations that have not reached this stage of development aspire to it as a desirable goal which, of course, only a very few countries have attained.

Even among nations sharing such aspirations, however, the serenity of relationships is troubled by circumstances beyond their control—often by the sheer weight of their traditions, the lack of understanding of the basic needs of freedom. Countries emerging from colonial tutelage are anxious to have shortcuts to progress. They lean heavily on those that are prosperous. And since altruism is rare among nations, as among individuals, aid and ideology get mixed up. The political consequences are not always happy. Thus even belief in coexistence is embittered by past memories and tensions.

Yet the towering fact is: Technological revolution, empowering the United States and the Soviet Union with nuclear weapons, forces them—and all the world—to fear destruction by this very power. Thomas Hobbes asserted that it was the fear of death that drove the individual to give up his natural state of war with all others and to accept limited freedom within the political community. Today the kindred fear—not of individual destruction but of universal destruction—is bringing nations together. It is true that the world's two concepts of coexistence mean totally different things: one based on conflict, the other on cooperation. They stem from different philosophies, and they lead to theories of relationships between states which differ from one another fundamentally. But today there are forces at work that compel nations to act together, in cooperation within the framework of an international organization—the United Nations. And over all the diversities of its members—so sharply different in basic traditions, political institutions, economic maturity—there rise the sovereign and unifying facts: the fear of annihilation—and a growing, urgent sense of community, for the sake of sheer survival.

This world society today is, obviously, pluralistic—culturally, politically, and economically—composed of communities in almost every stage of economic and political development. This diverse community is also torn between two political groups or alliances dominated by the Soviet Union and the United States—with both representing a high scientific and technical competence. The Soviet Union, having so swiftly moved from agrarian backwardness to technical competence, holds out great hope for the nascent democracies of Asia and Africa which have been left out in the race for progress. Its dictatorship techniques may have undermined democratic principles and spiritual values; but its material achievements have been spectacular, and its fascination is patently inescapable. On the other side, we have democratic societies where the traditions of freedom and long years of development have achieved the same material results in a laissez-faire atmosphere. Hence the new countries are compelled to make decisions that are not very easy—and that profoundly affect the roles of their own government within their economies.

If we examine present stages in the economic development of nations, three distinct patterns come to our view: namely, the free, the planned, and the socialist. All three vary in the degree of control and management exercised by the government over production and distribution. In the first there is more or less full freedom of private enterprise; in the second we have a mixed economy, with some important means of production owned by the state, and others left in private hands; and in the last every stage of production and distribution is owned and controlled by the state, and private enterprise is eliminated in various ways.

The historical experience of Western industrialized societies has been so special that it often hampers their understanding of peoples in Africa and Asia, having different histories and facing different problems. Even in these industrialized Western societies, with their traditions of liberalism and private enterprise, the gradually harmful consequences of unrestricted competition impelled the state to intervene in the regulation of conditions of work, in import and export policies, in opening markets—and in the building of vast colonial empires by small European states like England, France, Holland, Belgium, Italy, Germany, Spain, and Portugal. The pace and nature of industrial development in the metropolitan country were *dependent* on colonies for their raw materials. What would have been the rate of development of these European countries *without* the resources of colonies and colonial labor?

This is hardly a historical experience that can today be instructive to the so-called "underdeveloped" and developing economies of Asia and Africa—who so generally *were* colonies sustaining the economies of others. Most of these countries are still in the agricultural and pastoral stages of economic development. They must combat poverty, ignorance, and backwardness. Wealth and resources now concentrated in a few hands will have to be more equitably distributed for the general good of the community. And to effect this economic revolution, traditional habits of investment—and the indulgence in items like jewelry for conspicuous consumption—have to be changed. All such efforts to divert wealth to the most useful and productive channels requires some effective intervention of the state.

In such developing societies, therefore, the functions of the state are bound to be much greater than in developed economies. By their educational and industrial policies, planned with a view to achieving prescribed targets of production and development, the governments will have to go forward. They have to disturb violently, if necessary, the placid contentment of the people, wean them away from their traditional unproductive habits, inculcate in them an aversion to laziness, to poverty and ignorance, to disease and backwardness. This itself is a long and arduous process.

But even this is not enough. The state has to take responsibility in other matters as well. Investment and saving can be brought about only by the inculcation of new values. The needed capital for the development of resources cannot be left to the vagaries of the share market, nor can production be left to the kindness of nature or resources of private enterprise. The new economic policies will demand, to a large extent, state initiative and state action. It is not an abstract belief in socialism that compels all this—but sheer necessity.

In all these ways, in Asia and Africa, the transformation of society, which has happened elsewhere as a result of long and natural growth, will have to be brought about by conscious effort, conscious leadership—and through the instrument of the state. Inevitably this may mean restriction of private initiative and some infringement of individual rights. For the state is required to do two massive tasks: to provide essential tools necessary to any modern economy; and to inspire the people to abandon traditional habits, to work toward the economy's promise of a better and fuller life.

A further problem has arisen with countries newly independent. In almost all cases demand for independence has been closely connected with the demand for material welfare *and* freedom from economic domination, or exploitation, by foreign powers. Hence political independence is sought and fought for even at the price of an immediate economic disadvantage. Obviously a threat to independence is likely to come from too great economic dependence upon another for essential goods and services. The fear of this has compelled many countries to strive for self-sufficiency. The slogan "Defense is better than opulence" still has some meaning for these countries. And this struggle for self-sufficiency within newly independent countries brings on the intervention of the state to an uncontemplated degree. A government trying to push its economy to the take-off stage will need more initiative and more resources and will exercise more direct control than one that is well established and industrially advanced. Moreover, the desire to build up an egalitarian society compels these governments to pursue taxation policies to bridge the gulf that yawns between the rich and the poor—as well as industrial and labor policies to prevent the exploitation of man by man.

All these dilemmas—and aspirations—have naturally strained the economies of developing communities. With internal resources undeveloped or underdeveloped or inadequate, external aid has become indispensable. And this, in turn, inevitably precipitates problems of political independence in *new* form, if a nation wishes, as does India, to remain free of blocs, to design its own destiny—and assume its own responsibility—in the world.

The survival of humanity—and the acceptance of diversity—alike depend ultimately upon an understanding, a sense of responsibility, to which the *individual* citizen must be *educated*. Upon this all else depends.

Among us in India there is a well-known Sanskrit verse that says: "This is mine and this belongs to others. This is the way of thinking of small minds. For the large-hearted, the whole world is like one family." Today this is the problem of problems: to find the means to develop this attitude among the people and especially among those who have a part in making decisions for the entire world.

The relative degree of the obligation of the individual to society has been the topic of discussion from Greek times to this day. We may agree that the citizen's duty to the state is most simply expressed in two popular terms: civic duty and social responsibility. In a democratic society the citizen feels that he has a duty to the state that provides him with protection, freedom, and the needed amenities and services for a good life; and he also feels inspired by the thought that he could be of assistance to his community, in improving conditions of life and in helping solve the problems that face it. In India and other countries that have become free from colonial rule, it is not uncommon to find citizens constituting themselves into private voluntary organizations for social purposes. Thus, in the spheres of education or social services, normally the provinces of the state, actions and programs have been initiated and developed under private enterprise by individual citizens. The degree of responsibility of the citizens is in direct proportion to the state's concern for their well-being. We can expect people to safeguard only the things they have. Thus, well-to-do sections of society are likely to be more socially conscious and responsible than those overwhelmed with domestic problems—and the women more than the men, perhaps because any social disorder affects them more than other sections of the community. It is found that women are generally more socially conscious than men, and hence their increased participation is necessary for democracy. Participation in political affairs tends to heighten this responsibility. Each level of responsibility leads to the next step. Thus, the loyalties and responsibilities of the family develop into those of the community—and the state—and finally the world.

The citizen's sense of duty to the world—like his identification of himself with his nation—arises out of his identification of his nation's interest with that of the world community. Nationalism is regarded as an enemy of internationalism. Yet without nationalism it is difficult to talk of an international outlook. Our current task, in the words of Toynbee, "is to bring the disruptive force of nationalism under control and strengthen the tide in human affairs that is making towards

human unity." As the pursuit of common good and enduring
peace supersedes the bounds of nationality and nationalistic
outlook, then we have applied the meaning of the Sanskrit
verse, "For the large-hearted, the whole world is like one
family."

Just as mutual dependence is the source of mutual concern,
it is also the source of strength in the human family. So, too,
the interdependence of nations, large and small, so clearly
enunciated in the Charter of the United Nations, should
emphasize the need for coexistence. This should be the theme
of the educational adventures opening before us.

The ominous signs of division are all around us. Economic
nationalism itself is an expression of war psychosis. Our entire
life and activities too largely seem built on the fear that war
will overtake us some day and hence on the need to prepare
ourselves primarily by achieving economic self-sufficiency.
I come from a country that is passing through a stage of development depending on external aid. The economic objective of our plans is directed toward self-sufficiency. Can we
have political coexistence with economic isolation? Can we
hope to have an international cooperative society with each
country following economic policies that seem *inter alia* a
buildup for war?

The citizen's duty in this context is clear. The richness and
variety of human culture and civilization can no longer be
stifled in chauvinistic thinking and notions of racial superiority. Media of communication are such that news travels
faster even than human thought. We are told that the time
lag between presidential election and inauguration, in early
American history, was fixed by the time it took a horse car-
riage to travel from San Francisco to New York. Today the
Echo balloon takes only two and a half hours or less to circle
around the globe. In such a world it is sheer stupidity to think
in terms of boundaries and tariff walls, economic isolation
and self-sufficiency.

We must summon all faculties and all energies to draw the whole world out of the self-deception of the past—and to inspire people to face the future as members of the human family. The ultimate demand and need arise, not at the physical or economic level, but at the spiritual level. The framers of the UNESCO Charter said wisely that war is created in the minds of men and the defenses should also be created therein.

In this great task our educational institutions generally, and colleges and universities in particular, have a special responsibility. It is neither too late nor too early to teach our young that there is no natural conflict of cultures. People talk of defending their cultures; but what they mean is that there is a conflict of power. The exclusiveness of economic nationalism, the exclusiveness of political sovereignty, the exclusiveness of social status—all such outmoded and meaningless preconceptions must yield to the newer principles of cooperative effort, mutual aid, and peaceful coexistence. Traditional patterns of social cooperation fall short of modern needs. Today we are compelled to think in terms of the human family—the effort of all humanity and its well-being. And the issue is no longer a matter of practical expediency but of sheer necessity. We must make a choice—for survival.

13. The Individual and Society

SUSANNE K. LANGER

[UNITED STATES]

As a student of philosophy, rather than a social scientist, I should like to reflect philosophically on the meanings of our own words and on the implications of the statements we are entertaining. When the terms of a serious discourse are very exactly scrutinized—which is the first business of philosophy—many such terms that seemed to have quite clear and definite meanings prove to be vague and hard to define. They often have an emotional aura that makes the discourse persuasive; Professor Lovejoy has called this their good or bad "metaphysical pathos." But what should make one suspect that they are vague is, above all, that our most earnest thoughts lodged in those terms do not have immediate implications which lead to all sorts of specific elaborations and unexpected insights.

The key words in the topics proposed for our present discussion are "individual," "society," "creative experience," "science," and "art." Obviously we cannot examine them all now; but the first one—"individual"—is perhaps the most important and happens to be the one that I find the most problematical as a working concept.

The word "individual" has meant many things in many

contexts and even in a single one. In biology it generally means a creature that can carry on the basic life functions apart from other creatures, though it may prefer to be in company. Almost at once we are faced with certain anomalies: Is a hydra an individual? It and several companions have a common stomach and vascular system. Is the male of the marine worm *Bonnelia viridis* an individual? It is tiny, parasitic on the female, and spends its adult life in her uterus; yet in infancy it is independent, and unless it happens to sit down on the proboscis of a female (which the young like to do), it will become a female itself.* There are many other pseudo or semi-individuals. In speaking of human beings we often use the word "individual" in a laudatory sense: A true individual is morally responsible, serious, brave, and—oddly enough—more interested in others than in himself, etc. But when we speak of "*the* individual and society," we mean the average person, who has precious few such virtues. We slide from one concept to another, if you will even call such vague meanings concepts—for who has ever defined "the average person"?

The term "individual" is hard to define in a usable way, for it should be widely and yet precisely variable to fit many sorts of individual, from the problematical semi-individuals to Leviathan and Superman, from flowers in the crannied wall to poets who pluck them. But a noun with adjectives to characterize the varieties of things it covers expresses no working concept that relates the varieties and directs one to possible further ones. It is often more enlightening to work with terms that designate the *process* that engenders the thing in question and produces its various forms under different conditions.

The process that gives rise to individuals is immensely complex but may be broadly designated "individuation."

---

* Sinnot, Dunn, and Dobzhansky, *The Principles of Genetics*, 4th ed. (New York: McGraw-Hill, 1950).

Despite the complexity of all its manifestations it embodies a fundamental biological principle that operates in countless different circumstances, each of which makes the product, the individual, special if not unique. I find the concept of individuation much more useful than that of individuality, for reasons that I think every scientist can guess at once: A process has degrees and directions. A creature may be highly individuated in one direction and very little in another. For instance, robins are more closely involved with their parents in infancy—that is, less quickly individuated—than are geese: geese feed themselves and move under their own steam as soon as they are hatched, while baby robins acquire such in-dividual powers only gradually. But in another way robins are more individuated than geese: As adults they act sepa-rately in response to the environment, whereas geese act in chorus. If one goose gets up, they all do; if one sits down, they all sit down. There is no single factor of individuality present in different quantities in robins and geese, respec-tively. There are different forms of individuation: physical, as in the case of a mutant in a hereditary line, or—to stay nearer home—a person who looks like nobody else in the family; vital, like the cat who walks by himself; or mental. This last form is incomparably greater in human beings than in all other creatures but varies widely even among us. So do all the other forms.

Another advantage of starting with the concept of in-dividuation is that there is a converse process, which tends to hold a balance against it: The converse of individuation is called "involvement." I find that some baffling problems about the relations of individuals to society become negoti-able if they are treated in terms of individuation and involve-ment and the effects of any sudden or far-reaching change in the balance of those two biological principles.

It is customary, in talking about society, to begin with an idea of a particular society, usually a somewhat schematized imaginary tribe living in an unspecified wilderness and doing nothing but hunting big game, fighting exactly similar rival tribes, and dancing in triumph. The relation of a generalized member called "the individual" to this tribe is taken as the typical case, of which all actually known relations of members to social groups are variants.

That, however, is starting on a level that is already cultural and for scientific purposes has the drawback of being fictitious. I find it better to take the running start for my speculative leap further back and on somewhat harder ground. Let me say a few words about the pattern of individuation, and especially its limit, species involvement, in a more general frame of animal existence.

Among primitive creatures such as I have already mentioned, physical individuation may be visibly incomplete. Among some higher ones, for instance bees and ants, apparently complete individuals may not have the full complement of organs that would make them viable in isolation. Even in animals—including man—one form of species involvement remains essential: They cannot procreate without conjoint action. The offspring are physically made from parts of two parents. In most of the species, moreover, each birth is followed by a period during which the new life is dependent on one or both parents for its nurture. During this time its elementary behavioral patterns mature, the individual life unfolds.

That is what primarily I mean by saying each living creature is rooted in the life of an indefinitely long-lived stock and achieves a certain degree of individuation, typical of its kind, and variously furthered or fettered by its chance conditions. Not only its bodily structure but its impulses and the structure of its acts are inherited patterns. Animals are bound to repeat the repertoire of their ancestors because they are continuations of one long-evolved process. A cat is committed to feline activities, roving and essentially self-reliant, as a gopher is committed to his group life and his intense domesticity.

In the solitary animals (solitary except for episodes of mating and puerperium), individual existence has to be maintained by constant defense, escape, self-assertion, often in competition with other individuals of the same sort. In herd or hive animals certain influences that establish familiarity reduce this self-maintaining action within the group; but groups usually take a hostile attitude toward each other and toward members of other groups as parts of hostile colonies. That is to say, the phyletic stock is broken up into separate self-continuing *stocks*. The principle of individuation operates to make larger, continuing units, often with smaller subdivisions, of which the mortal individual is the final subunit.

Since we are concerned just now with human mortal individuals, let us turn to the human stock and its peculiarities, which have carried its individuating processes beyond those of any other species. Before the dawn of any cultural phenomena—before speech, dance, custom, or moral obligation— our ancestry was one of the primate stocks. Comparative anatomy puts that beyond question. But it must have been marked by some traits that were not found in the species that were most analogous to it, the precursors of our great apes. Above all, a highly developed brain was very probably a specialty of the *hominidae*. Such a trait is apt to give a radical turn to the further development of a species.

We do not know whether our kind in its purely animal stages lived in droves or in single families, pairing permanently as some forest animals do or mating promiscuously, but at times there must have been gathered hordes, because in scattered lives the all-important humanizing habit could probably not have taken root: the habit of speech. This activity springs more from the overgrown brain than from the creature's other anatomical specialties, though ear, larynx, and delicately mobile mouth parts are necessary for it. The origin of speech is unknown, but whatever guess we make at it rests on complex conditions which must have come together in this particular primate stock. We cannot enter into these questions here, except to note that the deepest and most momentous specialization, the thing that started humanity on its career as something else than an animal species, was the development of symbolic expression and symbolic understanding. Language has given us a means of communication with each other, but above all the power of thought, the awareness of many things at once which are not all given together in experience, and the power of conceiving things and conditions which do not exist at all. Our lives are always lived in a frame of possibility and conceptual assumptions which animals cannot share. They live in an environment variously felt; man lives in a world, which stays there when he sleeps or dreams or gives himself over to his fictitious conceptions.

The power of symbolism creates the need of symbols. We *need* to live in the conceptual frame of a world much larger than the environment we sensuously perceive, or realize from moment to moment in actual expectation, as animals do. We are partially freed from the operations of instinct, which are touched off by environmental factors, because we act in a world of thought. The smallness or greatness of a creature's ambient is the measure of its individual freedom— that is, the directions and the extent to which its individuation can go. In accordance with our mentally widened and mentally structured world, it is our mental life that has the greatest scope for individuation. The human individual is essentially a mental being.

To a creature with a need for symbolic expression and a constant tendency to find symbolic values, nature furnishes symbols of everything emotionally important. The naturally engendered and isolated tribe, be it large or small, which corresponds to the separate hive or pack of animals maintains its integrity even against its own kind, for man becomes the symbol of something he could not otherwise grasp: humanity. Many tribes call themselves by a name that means "man." Yet they cannot consciously imagine mankind as such. This symbolic function of the tribe is unconsciously accepted. Our unconsciously accepted symbols are the most powerful; in conscious experience they figure not as symbols but as sacred things. Often the tribe itself is symbolically represented by a totem, a divine dynasty, a patron god, or even the god's name, which is invested with the character of holiness. Humanity is too vast to be directly conceived, it has to be symbolized; but it is this symbolic value that makes the natural unit a social unit, for humanity is more than a species: It is society, and its continuity is history. The actively recognized involvement of each person with the social unit to which he belongs attests and upholds his involvement with his kind, expressed particularly by the commitments that are made for him by his birth into that unit—be it a tribe, a clan, a class, or any other hereditary frame.

I said before, though only in passing, that symbolic conception freed us from the operation of instinct. An animal's instinctive activity is its lifelong, actual, and ineluctable involvement in the way of its kind, its participation in the life of the stock. If its instincts failed or wavered, it would be undone, for it has no other mechanism for initiating any action. A robin without its nest-building instinct would not know what to do about its eggs; it might even be unable to produce them. Nothing serves better to show the reciprocal relation between the principles of individuation and involvement than animal instinct. Animals act by instinct—a lifelong commitment to the ways of their kind—to preserve themselves as individuals. The particular life form of the stock is at once the limit and the guarantee of their separate existence.

In man, the animal instincts are too much reduced to be reliable starters or guides of group action or personal behavior. What has suppressed them and gradually displaced them is the high activity of the brain, the special ability to operate with symbols which is manifested in conception, speech, and speculative thought on all levels, from simple, practical cause-and-effect reasoning to the most difficult abstract theories.

Is man, then, exempt from the need of involvement with his own kind? Is he physically, practically, and emotionally self-sufficient? Physically, no more than other mammals. His beginning is in sexual union, his infancy long and completely dependent. Practically, he can do fairly well as Robinson Crusoe—but so can most animals. Emotionally he is certainly not self-sufficient. Loneliness is one of his hazards. But—as a great biologist (Pflüger) has said—in nature "the source of the need is the source of the fulfilment of the need." The mental function of symbolization, which augments the scope of our world so no system of instinctive responses could meet its demands, and therefore breaks the most constant bond of the individual to its kind, makes this bond largely unnecessary to us by providing symbols of our participation in the greater life of mankind, symbols of humanity and of our involvement in it. We can push our individuation beyond the limits to which any other creature's can go, without losing the balance between individuation and involvement, because we have symbolic substitutes for the natural bonds which we give up. And I think it may be said that we can afford to become individualized just to the extent that we can replace the natural ties that used to hold us to our kind by symbolic ones: obligations, recognition of hereditary commitments, pieties, sanctions, honors, and, above all, the diverse rites of holy communion.

Everything I have said so far is by way of introduction, but so it is. One trouble with philosophizing is that before you reach any interesting implications, you have to analyze so many lumpy ideas. Perhaps we had better take inventory of the notions I have tried to clarify so far, because they are needed before I can present you with the view of the human individual's position in society today, to which I hope you will give consideration.

An *individual* is hard to define, as there are partially or vaguely individual beings, and even among unmistakably individual creatures their individuality rests on different, sometimes incommensurable traits.

It is more profitable to study the processes of *individuation*, which are quite various, take different directions, go on at different rates of speed, and attain different degrees.

Individuation is one of the basic and ubiquitous biological principles, manifested in all of animate nature and taking the most diverse forms.

One scientific advantage of the concept of individuation is that its negative is not just the privative concept of nonindividuation, but an important condition, sometimes even a reverse process: the *involvement* of a creature with the living stock from which its individuation springs.

The *stock* is the original living entity of indefinite duration. No individual creature can originate or survive without being to some degree involved with the parent stock.

Involvement can take many forms. Procreation, and in higher forms of life the sexual union preceding procreation, constitute the most elementary, physical rootedness of each individual in the continuum of life here called the stock. Repetition of basic forms known as *inheritance* is another bond. It may be bodily form or behavioral. Animals run true to type even in elaborate behavior, the *instinctual* pattern.

Man differs from all other creatures in the form and function of his brain. The cerebral function that sets him apart more than anything else is his use of symbols to formulate and hold ideas. Symbolic activity begets language, religion, art, logical insight, and the power of carrying on a train of abstract thoughts, or reasoning. All imagination requires symbols. All conception is symbolic.

Animals depend on their instincts for self-preservation. Man cannot rely on any built-in behavior patterns. The range of his possible actions has been so enormously widened by his conceptual powers—imagination, cognition, and speculation—that no inherited repertoire could fit the contingencies of his world.

But the natural ties to his kind which he loses with the great growth of his mind are replaced by that same mental power which broke them, the power of symbolization; and we can afford to carry our individuation just as far as symbols of our social involvement hold the balance against it.

So now, after all these preliminaries, we come close to the problem I am setting out so circuitously to discuss, the problem that bears directly on topics of this conference: What has happened to the relations of individuals to society that makes us aware of them as never before and makes us feel vaguely if not acutely that something is wrong between them?

Again I must ask you to look at one of the most general patterns in nature, the evolution of higher forms from primitive ones to vital activity. The lowest organisms have no special organs. They react as a whole to light, temperature, and even food. Any part of an amoeba can momentarily become anything, make any response in the creature's repertoire. In higher stages of life, special organs react selectively to the different kinds of stimuli. Still further up the evolutionary ladder we find these organs highly elaborated into complexes of subordinate parts. For instance, the organ of hearing begins as a mechanism for picking up massive vibrations passing through water, earth, or air. Gradually it becomes specialized for sound waves in the air. The inner ear is elaborated so that different frequencies of these waves register as different tones in our hearing, and we have a gamut of distinguishable pitches. The breaking up of the nervous mechanism into special subunits goes on until its function becomes too complicated to be practicable. As long as the vibrations come at rates of hundreds per second, and even up to a couple of thousands, the ear can react differently to slightly different numbers. If we take the sound of 440 vibrations per second as the orchestra's A, 436 or 444 will sound "out of tune." The ear distinguishes such differences. But when the frequency goes up into the thousands, it can no longer perceive differences of 4 vibrations per second. Then a major shift takes place: The perceptible differences are no longer gradations on a unit scale, but jump by thousands. This is a shift to a new principle of operation, a redeployment of the subunits, a simplification of the process at a new level of response. It is like a gearshift.

I think a universal principle of evolution is the differentiation of forms to the smallest functional subunits and, after that, a *shift of functions* to new, unpredictably different, big subunits, made out of the smallest ones by a new process which starts here: *integration*. A reversal of the progressive individuation takes place. Old processes give way to new modes of operation proper to the newly integrated organic structures.

Now let me draw the moral of all these stories. The same pattern found in organic evolution—that is, in the development of individual beings—obtains in the development of the living stock as one indefinitely long life. We may as well come right to the human stock. We find progressive differentiation, breaking up into subunits, various races of man—a breaking up that we usually cannot trace, but reconstruct after the fact; then further divisions into smaller subunits effected mainly by circumstances that isolate or assemble hereditary lines, forming natural groups—tribes, families—sometimes confluent lines, equally natural expanded groups, such as clans and peoples, nations. The constitutive units in such groups usually keep some of their identity, as the twelve tribes of Israel and the various familial stocks of the Vikings did for a long time. On such historic foundations, dynasties, classes, castes, and other social divisions are based.

A society is easier to apprehend than the entire human stock ranging back to immemorial time. A tribe has a remembered ancestry, a living membership, a future foreshadowed in the growing children. For such symbolmongers as human beings are, everything that has any permanent identity tends to acquire symbolic value and be used to embody a greater conception—that is, to mean more than meets the eye; primitive symbols are made spontaneously out of the forms that nature provides, including forms of behavior; and the social subunit—the tribe, the clan, the church, or the caste with which a person most ardently identifies himself—is his symbol of the greater life that enfolds him, all humanity. He does not know this; in his consciousness the group is all that claims him. But the fact is that he can shift his explicit allegiance from one body to another—from his tribe to his race, or to a mystic brotherhood, or even his family—and somehow the sense of it is always the same: a greater life. The symbolic office of the greater body to which he gives himself is manifested only in his emotion toward it, which would be inexplicable if that body were a purely practical arrangement to implement common affairs.

In the long history that lies equally behind each one of us, the most persistent and active individuating tendencies have been manifested in the evolution of the brain. In place of instinctual behavior, men have developed a form of behavior that derives largely from imagination, cogitation, and judgment, with a conscious moment of *intention* before the body goes into action. This is moral freedom—freedom from the narrow confines of animal reactions in which there are only small options and immediate decisions, no resolutions, policies, or obligations. We are still carrying on our personal individuation. The fact here in point is that throughout the long ages in which human freedom was evolved, men have held to their symbols of that essential and good human bondage that keeps the tiny death-bound life a part of the greater life of our kind. There seems to be normally a long "organismic" or organism-life phase of society in which special offices, functions, and stations become articulated and established by more or less natural processes: "elders" governing the community, or families achieving ascendency and handing it on by inheritance, or men credited with mystical powers founding a priesthood and making some provision for its continuity which becomes automatic. These forms evolve somewhat as tissues in a developing organism become specialized by their position, external exposure, or proximity to the source of general nutrition, so they form special organs through their particular involvement with the whole. In human society the fighting power is naturally vested in the men from youth to middle life, in whom aggressive impulses, competition, pride, and exuberance combine to make a warrior caste without any conscious design.

Every high culture seems to have gone through such an evolution. Its height is a dynastic absolute monarchy correlated with a strong priesthood, sometimes meeting in the royal personage itself. This structure may be maintained for a long time, because it serves to symbolize the organic unity of human life on a large scale, and permits the long slow process of mental individuation for which we need the assuring symbol of our security in a greater living whole. The emotional expression of that assurance—devoutness and loyalty—is likely to be most complete and ardent in the monarchical, perhaps theocratic phase of national life.

After that the operation of the individuating principle in the greater whole, the society, begins to outrun the tempo of man's symbol-making capacity; the breaking up of the royal and ecclesiastic order by more and more autonomy of its inherent parts produces legislative and military councils, separate religious bodies, economic power groups not allied with any high and venerated authority. The emotional effect on people as individuals is that the holiness goes out of all institutions. For many persons today, some small sectarian church of their own choosing and the family based on holy matrimony are the only things still regarded as sacred. But adherence to a faith is no longer mandatory, and although marriage is still supposed to be lifelong, divorce is generally tolerated. Only a generation or two ago a divorced person was considered a disgrace to his family, and children of broken homes bore a stigma, though not quite as much as the poor waifs born out of wedlock. Today they are humanely accepted even in so-called "good society." In fact—this is the important upshot of it all—in the more advanced parts of the Western culture which derives from Europe, *we no longer visit the sins of the fathers on the children.* Please do not conclude that I think we should still do so; I am sure we should not. But that does not mean that people never should have done so, or that nothing is lost by the change.

I think what has happened to society, and is still happening, is that the individuation of its parts has all but reached its limit. Society is breaking up into its ultimate units—single individuals, persons. Many things could be adduced in evidence of this momentous fact if we only had the time. But the fact is that in our Western culture—which is, unfortunately, the only one I know—each individual really stands alone, without support of status or even family background. The recognition of such personal singleness is expressed in the basic principle of democratic government—"each counts for one and only one." Our magistrates are charged to mete out justice "without respect for persons." It is "man for himself" in our world.

We are witnessing the beginning of a vast change in

society, nothing less than a biological shift of functions to new structures. The organismlike phase of society, in which more and more subordinate forms become articulated, is reaching its close; the new structures which are already in the making—and, indeed, have long been so—are products of *integration,* new wholes made out of very small ones, even out of the ultimate units. In society such integral forms are *institutions.* In the past, institutions were based on the natural social articulations and were essentially recognized and sanctioned natural products. In the future they will have to spring more and more from the higher mental processes that are peculiar to man: conscious planning and ruling.

Meanwhile we are caught in the turbulence of the shift. With the fast breakup of natural social units our inherited symbols of humanity are failing, and countless people to whom this is happening feel—but cannot understand—their loss of the sense of involvement, which makes the world seem like a meaningless rat race in which they are reduced to nothingness, alone in life and in death. They turn desperately back to religions they had let go or to exotic cults that promise a new mode of salvation, condemn their actual world as false, reject what seems to hurry the fragmentation of society—science, technology, and the cultivation of reason that begot those advances—and long to return to the unconscious, instinct-guided self-realization of animals, or at least to the tribal pieties they attribute to unknown savages. Meanwhile they do not know that the most dramatic rejection of social involvement lies in their repudiation of the onerous things civilized life visits on them, for our strongest bond to our kind is the acceptance of commitments we did not make, commitments made for us by the circumstances of our birth on the decrees of our elders. No matter how much we want to stop the progress of individuation, our own acts hurry it. Most people today, and especially the thoughtful and serious ones, feel that they are not bound by any commitment they have not made themselves. The most spectacular version of this doctrine is that new governments superseding old, traditional, obsolete ones may repudiate obligations and agreements entered into by their predecessors.

The loss of emotional security with the shattering of our natural symbols—hurried by the two wars which have uprooted millions of people—is patent, and any reintegration of life on new lines—so new that no one can even hazard a guess at its design—is in its infancy, and it will be long before it provides forms that can take on deep social significance and become our symbols of humanity and its place in nature.

14. The Future
of Education

VERA MICHELES DEAN

[UNITED STATES]

Ｔ HE ECONOMIC and technological facts of life give
our world today a character and a stamp that none can doubt
or erase. Industrialization is on the march across the earth.
The pace of change is irreversible—and quickening. Isolation for any nation or people, however large or powerful, has
become unthinkable fantasy. And the historic result is the
interdependence of all peoples of the world, to a degree never
before known in all the story of mankind.

What does this new interdependence mean to education?
It means most clearly that the educator must take into account the myriad changes brought about in our various
societies. He must strive to guide the direction of these
changes. And he must assume responsibility for the development of the mind and character of the individuals who will
be building the world of the future, long after this generation
has passed from the scene.

Education in such a world—as I see it—must be regarded
not as a series of compartments of learning but as a kind of
seamless web—as total preparation for life for men and
women at *all* levels: in primary and secondary schools, col-

188

leges and universities, technical institutions, adult education groups, in technical training of all kinds.

We ask ourselves: What is the goal of such education? From time immemorial the dedicated teacher has always hoped to educate not this or that fragment of an individual, but the whole human being. This task remains unchanged in the electronic age. Admittedly it is far more difficult to educate the whole individual today, when the problems of industrialization and the responsibilities of democracy have made life far more complex than it is, let us say, in the days of Plato or of Leonardo da Vinci. Nor is this all: Anything we may do in education today, in this jet-speed age, may become obsolete tomorrow. Thus we must not think simply of what is worth doing at all levels of education now, in 1961—but of what may be useful at least a decade from now.

This means that we are all rather a little like the astronauts who are being trained for travel into outer space. We must prepare ourselves and the students whom we are to guide, for travel into spheres we ourselves cannot always claim to know. Naturally we have to start from the known. But it is essential for us to anticipate the unknown and perhaps even the unknowable. At the same time, while the future poses such challenges, the past bequeaths rare and great problems. For we must reconstruct education, both in the West and in the non-Western countries, amid the destruction, or at least erosion, of old values and of traditional relationships in the family and in the community.

All this is indeed a task to stagger the imagination of the most daring among us. Some feel faint-hearted at the prospect and are beset by doubts and anxieties. But let us take as our own motto for this venture an adaptation by James Thurber of the remark made by Winston Churchill: This is an awful and magnificent century to live in, and I wouldn't miss it.

That is the way I feel about it: Let us think of this task not as a burden but as an unrivaled opportunity for making the most effective use of the human resources now becoming available all around the world.

These human resources are being made available by a host of changes through all the world: the release of ancient peoples, with great civilizations behind them, from the colonial rule of Western powers; all the new prospects of producing more food, more consumer goods, more machines, more homes; all the new opportunities for the exchange of goods, of skills, of capital—made possible by national and international agencies and the creation of regional and world economic units. Think of the dazzling prospects open to us to draw upon the entire world storehouse of spiritual and intellectual riches: of religions, of philosophies, of art, of music, and of literature.

Some of us must fear that interdependence and rapid communications and all the new technological devices making the world one—all these may also make it a dreary world, a world of conformity in which all the fascinating diversities of peoples and cultures will be smothered by worldwide imitation, if not of Western pattern, then of industrial patterns as presented by both the West and the Communist world. For the Communists in Russia, and in my opinion also in China, are the "Westernizers" who are altering ancient civilizations according to the new technological patterns. All this—it is often feared—may impoverish the spirit of man, even while seemingly improving his physical well-being.

This, to my mind, is a danger that need not come to pass.

Every culture today, as independence comes to one nation after another, is free to draw from the world's common heritage whatever ideas, skills, practices it may require. It does not need to succumb to blind imitation of any one culture. It is free to preserve, and should preserve, those values and traditions of its own past which it wants for its own future. In short, there is an opportunity for selection by every nation, and we know that this is possible because we have seen it done by several non-Western nations, notably Japan. At the same time each independent culture and society has something to *give to* the common heritage. No longer is it necessary for the technologically less developed countries, once subject to colonial rule, to accept unquestioningly the cultural patterns of the colonizing power. And as *all* peoples give their special gifts to the world's resources of spirit, mind, and skill, they will be helping to achieve the equality of all peoples, by fully expressing the dignity of each.

In this new interdependent world what are the qualities we must seek and inspire through our education? To go back to the astronauts—who offer so fascinating an experiment in education—they have been carefully selected for qualities of both mind and body, for endurance as well as resourcefulness, for physical stamina as well as for mental adaptability. What kind of human beings do we want—to be able to move into the new spheres we may not even yet know?

Should intellect be their outstanding characteristic? This may sound like a peculiar question for any educator to ask. But I am not convinced at this point that intellect alone, unless accompanied by other qualities, is going to be the quality that will carry people to greatness in the unknown world of the future. Must we not also stress training in terms of ethical principles? of character? of personality? As one looks back upon one's students—as one looks back upon life— I think it becomes obvious that the gift of love in a human being is just as important as the gift of the intellect; and without the gift of human warmth the intellect can be a very arid thing indeed.

Many talents can be developed by the educator. Many skills can be taught in vocational schools. But there are also qualities that neither books nor machines can give to the individual. Imagination, humor, patience—here are qualities essential to all dealings between nations and peoples, all international work in our world. And there have to be other qualities: integrity and courage. These are indispensable to the living of a responsible and productive life among the temptations and dangers of the fast-paced modern world, among rapidly changing standards of conduct. And finally, and vitally, there is the quality of faith—faith in one's own religious concepts, a faith freely held and freely practiced. For—in the fine phrase of Heraclitus quoted by our friend from Greece, Ketty Stassinopoulou—there is not much value to eyes and ears without a soul behind them.

The qualities of the individual we want to be educated serve also to help us identify the qualities we need in the educators.

The teacher, it goes without saying, must have knowledge, but it is crucial that he be honest about the use of his knowledge, about his own beliefs—honest in the classroom as well as outside. He must act as a responsible citizen, if he is going to inspire those he teaches to be responsible. I question some of my academic colleagues when they complain that all the students are so apathetic, or that what all the students want is security. When teachers make these laments, I am inclined to ask them: Are *you* active in the affairs of your community or of your nation? Are *you* taking risks? Are *you* possibly too concerned with security? The simple truth is that it takes a brave teacher to inspire bravery in his students.

I think we might all agree that a teacher must abstain from sheer political agitation, but he should be free—in fact, he should be encouraged—to participate actively in the affairs of his community, his nation, and the world community. Moreover, the teacher, if he is worth his salt at all, is a man who looks to the future and wants to improve whatever he is working on. Thus, by definition, he is a reformer. He is looking toward better ways of thinking, better ways of teaching,

THE FUTURE OF EDUCATION / 193

better ways of making a society. But let us hope that we shall not expect him to be a missionary. I, at least, prefer him not to be a missionary, if this means trying to convert others to his ideas. Rather, it seems to me, he should be ready to share his ideas with others, to understand the ideas of the people with whom he deals, but not to try to impose his thoughts on those he teaches.

In the light of the contribution that the teacher can and should make to society, he is plainly entitled to the respect of society—and to something more. He is entitled to remuneration that gives him freedom to think, to study, to create—and thus to act in the role he must fill effectively, the role of trailblazer for the society in which he lives.

The teacher, in short, must be more than one who educates. He must be a *leader*, as the teacher, in fact, usually was in ancient societies. As such he can do immeasurably much to help heal the world's scars and divisions. He can creatively share the responsibility for reconstructing a social order whose ancient values and traditional beliefs are being destroyed or eroded by the surge of new ideas and practices. He can do so by realizing—and helping others around him to realize—that in human society, as in nature, nothing needs to be irretrievably lost, even if much may be transformed. The tree that sheds its leaves in the autumn will turn green again—another spring. It is thus, or can be, in all parts of our world.

Consider, for example, the dissolution of the joint family in Asia, Africa, or the Middle East. The dissolution of the joint family certainly brings losses: It brings dislocation; it brings pain to many individuals, a sense of insecurity. But are there not gains? It also brings about the end of parental tyranny, the end of woman's subjection to a sometimes less than gracious mother-in-law, the removal often of repressive restrictions on new ideas and new contacts.

Or, turn to the United States. Here, in a technologically

developed society, the growth of urban life, the financial
pressures upon the mother to work, the shortage of after-
school facilities—all such things help to bring about juvenile
delinquency, gang warfare, undue dependence on mechanical amusements of often dubious quality offered by movies
and television. But is there nothing good that comes out of
urban life? Of course there can be great good. If imagina-
tively handled, urban living brings new opportunities not
enjoyed in rural areas for children of underprivileged families
(like the Puerto Rican families in New York City) to come
into contact with untold cultural riches: museums, theaters,
concerts, organized sports.

Thus everywhere in the world today where there is change
—and this means *everywhere*—there is also opportunity, for
both teacher and taught, to help make change creative and
not destructive. And everywhere the exact nature of the
opportunity (like the nature of the change) is *different*. It is
impossible to lay down precise rules about the relative value
of primary, secondary, university, or vocational education in
any nation, at any time. Every nation has its own special
needs, its own traditions, its own aspirations for the future.
It alone can decide the kind of education it wants at a given
time. It alone can make its own list of educational priorities.
Concretely, the developed nations of the West can offer only
such aid to the nations of Asia, Africa, the Middle East, and
Latin America as they want to have. It is not for the West
to decide what should be done in the non-Western world.

Sometimes our friends in the non-Western countries are
naturally beset by an overwhelming awareness that they
seem compelled, in their educational and social progress, to
have to try to do everything at once. Can you do primary
and secondary and university and vocational work all at the
same time? Can you, at the same time, bring in technology
and cultivate the arts? How *can* it be done?

The problem is not a new one. It was felt even in the

American republic, in the early days of the founding fathers. John Adams, in a letter to his wife written from Paris in 1788, had this to say:

I wish I could describe to you in greater detail the beauties of art which I am seeing in Versailles and in Paris. But [he said] let me not pause to discuss this because we have other things to do in the United States. It is not indeed the fine arts which our country requires. The useful mechanical arts are those which we have occasion for in a young country as yet simple and not far advanced in luxury, although perhaps much too far for age and character. I could fill volumes with descriptions of palaces and temples of paintings, sculptures, tapestry, porcelain, etc., etc., etc., if I had time, but I could not do this without neglecting my duty. I must study politics and war, that my sons may have liberty to study mathematics and philosophy. My sons ought to study mathematics and philosophy, geography and natural history, and naval architecture, navigation, commerce and agriculture in order to give their children a right to study painting, poetry, music, architecture, statuary, tapestry and porcelain.

The problem of educational priorities, then, is hardly a new one. Nor has it been confined to any particular areas or societies. In every country the cost of education, as we all know, is great and will become still greater as more and more citizens seek, or are encouraged to seek, educational opportunities. Again, each nation must decide where and how it prefers to spend its limited funds—the funds it has at home or the funds obtained through foreign aid, either from individual governments or from grants from international agencies. The choice, admittedly, is far more difficult for the technologically new countries than for those that already have a broad base for industrial development. It is hard for India and Nigeria, for example, to decide whether limited funds are to be spent on education—or for steel mills or dams or industry. But if it is any comfort to our friends from non-Western countries, they should know that we are struggling now to make choices between spending money on cars with fins, cosmetics, alcohol, and other such things; or on expansion of industrialization, or even on the manufacture of armaments; or on education at all levels. In these difficult choices perhaps a more rational answer would more often be given if one basic concept were better understood: that education is an *investment*—an investment in human resources—not just an expenditure.

The clearest task before teachers in every nation, of course, is to make decisions about the studies to be included in the curriculum. This, of course, is not so simple a task as it appears, and there can be infinite differences of opinion about the proper place of politics or economics, the role of science, the humanities, or the social sciences in any curriculum. I shall state merely what seems to me a general need: to achieve *balance* among the humanities, science, and the social studies. There should be less competition and more correlation among them. To my mind, this suggests the importance for the future of increasing interdepartmental work at all levels of education. This involves not only colleges and universities but also teams of teachers in elementary and high schools, so that each group of teachers and scholars may profit through interchanges of ideas, practices, and discoveries. Thereby they might better hope to communicate to the student something often lacking in our highly diversified society: a sense of *synthesis* in intellectual life.

A like need for synthesis brings the educator another challenge: the endeavor to make an effective blend of the contributions of the West and the non-West to a common heritage. In the United States we are still only on the threshold of giving our students serious knowledge of Africa, Asia, the Middle East, Latin America. Of course, we have excellent work and programs in graduate institutions, but far, far more has to be done in schools and colleges. Perhaps there is a real contrast in the problem in the non-Western countries. They may, in fact, wish to *reduce* the wealth of material on Western areas which has been brought into their curriculums during the long colonial period. I was very much struck—when I had the pleasure of teaching briefly at the Indian School of International Studies in New Delhi—to find how much of the curriculum of their university was still crowded with materials about Britain, British history, and British institutions, but relatively little about India itself. And even for my graduate students there had been remarkably little study of neighbors of India, including China. From such neighboring non-Western countries there had been a kind of isolation, imposed by the colonial rulers—not only physically or politically but also in many respects intellectually. Here, again, is a situation that can greatly be helped by the interchange of ideas between the West and the non-West—with educators in both areas putting greater emphasis upon new studies, appropriate to the different areas, yet all recognizing the new interdependence of our world.

The matter of *who* is to be taught poses another challenge: the educator must recognize an obligation not only to his students but also to the *adults* in his society. And in meeting this challenge the educator must not look down his nose on all the devices for education offered by the technological age, from the teaching machines to television. I am the last person to say that American television is admirable, but the fact remains that a machine of itself is neither good nor bad. What is good or bad is the use that is made of it.

The educator should be eager to participate in all processes of adult education that can be offered and used. By such participation he will advance the growth of the pluralistic society, a society that, by definition, presents a multiplicity of difficult choices to citizens at all levels—local, national, and international. There appeared not long ago a cartoon in the *New Yorker* suggesting how we feel about this—a cartoon presenting two communists in front of the Kremlin,

saying to each other, "That's the trouble with democratic society—decisions, decisions, decisions." True enough—and how
are you going to make decisions unless you have some educated knowledge to guide you? This is where the educator
can step in—right into the marketplace.

At a time when the people's needs are so great, the university must not be an ivory tower. It should extend a welcome to all men and women who wish to make use of its
resources, of human talent, its libraries, its laboratories.
There is a hunger for education throughout the world, a
hunger that is almost a physical need. It is felt not only in
the newly emerging countries but also in the advanced countries as well. To meet this hunger, to feed this admirable
appetite, our universities should be open day and evenings
the year round, not only for relatively brief periods each day
nor merely for seven or eight months a year. Universities
are citadels of tomorrow where all citizens can gradually
build—together—new intellectual security among the inse-
curities of a changing world.

In these various ways the educator may help to ease and
reconcile one of the great conflicts of our time: the conflict
between the claims and demands of the welfare state and
those of the individual craving freedom. This conflict, in
varying form and degree, stirs in all societies today.

It is unrealistic, surely, to think that any of us can now go
back to the past—to restore the old agrarian society everywhere being rapidly changed by modern technology. It is
surely unrealistic to expect that we could reconstruct the
family as it was in earlier ages—not only the center of family
life but also, in effect, a welfare unit for all its members. Instead, we have to face the new problems of this urban society
with new approaches. We need, in short, to discover ways of
combining individual freedom with concern for the welfare
of all citizens. As Dr. Hannah Arendt suggested imagina-
tively in our discussions, this reconciling of the welfare state

THE FUTURE OF EDUCATION / 199

and individual freedom could be greatly helped by our recognizing that we must have varying degrees of freedom at different levels within a society. The essential roots of freedom are not gravely at stake, for example, in decisions about the processes of industrial production. The place of freedom is obviously utterly different in the political processes. And the greatest freedom of all, which must be defended at all costs, is the freedom of the intellect—the freedom that cannot be surrendered without democracy being transformed into a totalitarian police state. Precisely here, perhaps, the educator can make perhaps the greatest contribution of all: by defending without surcease the right of every human being to hold and express his own ideas, no matter how unpopular these ideas may be at a given time in a given society.

Finally, there is the greatest of all conflicts to challenge the educator: the conflict between the claims of the nation and those of the international community. It is essential to preserve in every nation its values of spirit and mind—all that it has developed, nurtured, and cherished throughout the ages. This is the stuff and substance of human existence. But it is at the same time imperative to make the individual profoundly aware that he is a part not only of his own local community and nation but also of a world whose every event affects him in all aspects of his being—his life, his hopes, his very chances of survival.

The teacher, if he is to serve in this role, must learn to understand the hopes and fears of people outside his experience, even if he disapproves of their ideas and practices. To understand is not to condone, but neither is it rational to condemn other peoples without understanding. If we are to live in an interdependent world, we shall have to accept the fact that there are many different ideologies, many different religions, customs, traditions, ways of life. I am not suggesting—although some of my conferees may not agree with me—that we should emphasize the idea of coexistence. The word has acquired too many meanings: We all hope to co-exist, as distinct from being blown to pieces in a nuclear holocaust, but this is not the same notion of coexistence as the Communists suggest by their policies and struggles around the earth, from the Congo to Laos. What I am emphasizing is simply the plain and urgent need to develop all the understandings and sensitivities vital to the growth of a world community.

This world community, today represented by the United Nations and other international agencies, is admittedly still feeble, still not adequate to deal with the enormous tasks being thrust upon it. But it is unthinkable to despair about the future of the United Nations. The task before us—and there is no other choice—is to proceed with the completion of the edifice, the structure of an international organization in which all nations, no matter what their technical development or what their education, are equals.

Here, it seems to me, is the basic and most crucial task of the educator in the years ahead—the great educational work of *integration*. Just as the small urban family is to be integrated into the local community, and the community into the nation, so we must look ahead to the integrating of the nation in the international society. Indeed, this challenge puts before us prospects and adventures as intellectually stimulating as any that the astronauts may meet in outer space. I am sufficiently mundane to assume that even if the astronauts reach Venus or Mars, there will not be too much for them or for us on all the planets. And the rest of us will have to live on earth and, therefore, should make every effort to improve our common life upon this planet.

I would not want to leave you with the idea that either this conference's participants or I are hopelessly sentimental people. I myself would be the last to say that if we do create a workable world community, this will be the end of conflict and the coming of perfect peace. I do not believe there is such a thing as perfect peace, except in cemeteries.

No, there will always be conflict. But the essential truth I would put in the words of a recent musical play based on Voltaire's *Candide*. Those of you who have seen this lovely play, which stayed much too short a time on Broadway, saw the end of another great ideological struggle in modern history: Candide returns to the Waldfeld with his master Pangloss, who held that everything is for the best in this best of all possible worlds. And when Pangloss says to him, "Now let us sit here among the ruins and talk about perfect harmony," Candide replies, "Let us not talk about perfect harmony, because there is no such thing." And then he adds, "But let us try, before we die, to make sense of life."